"In *A Wondrous Mystery*, Geoff Chang has collected Spurgeon's Christmas sermons to help us keep our eyes fixed on Jesus. I can think of no better way to respond to the busyness of Christmas than to slow down and meditate on the glories of the incarnation."

Juan R. Sanchez, Senior Pastor, High Pointe Baptist Church, Austin, TX; coauthor of *Reaching Your Child's Heart*

"Spurgeon's captivation with Christ bubbles over as he dwells upon the incarnation. Combining deep thought and deep delight, his studies of the Son of God taking our nature settle our faith and stir our love. These sweet extracts, judiciously chosen and helpfully introduced, reveal and stimulate reverence and joy rooted in the wonder of Immanuel—God with us."

Jeremy Walker, Pastor, Maidenbower Baptist Church, Crawley, UK; speaker; author; *From the Heart of Spurgeon* podcast host

"No preacher of God's Word speaks to me more powerfully than Charles Spurgeon. His are the words of an old friend, though sadly many of my other friends don't yet know him. Many thanks to Geoff Chang for giving us Spurgeon's rich insights into Christ's incarnation."

Randy Alcorn, Author of *Heaven*, *We Shall See God*, and *Grieving with Hope*

"While some mines quickly exhaust their stores of precious metals, others keep giving forever. And so too do the works of Charles Spurgeon. This book is a collection of treasures that will bless you this Christmas or any Christmas."

Tim Challies, Pastor; speaker; author of *Seasons of Sorrow*

"*A Wondrous Mystery* contains pure gold from Spurgeon's treasury of teaching on the incarnation. Far from being an opponent of Christmas celebrations, Spurgeon joined them. Though opposing religious superstition, he championed the Christmas holiday. This volume by Geoff Chang will delight you, deepen your theology of Christmas, and be a helpful tool for family worship."

Ray Rhodes Jr., Author of *Susie: The Life and Legacy of Susannah Spurgeon* and *Yours, till Heaven: The Untold Love Story of Charles and Susie Spurgeon*

A Wondrous Mystery

A Wondrous Mystery

Daily Advent Devotions

CHARLES H. SPURGEON

EDITED BY GEOFFREY CHANG

newgrowthpress.com

New Growth Press, Greensboro, NC 27401
newgrowthpress.com
Copyright © 2024 by Geoffrey Chang

Cover Design: Faceout Books, faceoutstudio.com
Interior Typesetting and E-book: Lisa Parnell, lparnellbookservices.com

ISBN 978-1-64507-433-5 (Print)
ISBN 978-1-64507-434-2 (eBook)

Library of Congress Cataloging-in-Publication Data on File

Printed in the India

31 30 29 28 27 26 25 24   1 2 3 4 5

To my parents

Contents

Contents

Introduction

Thanks to English Puritanism in the seventeenth century, Christmas was largely forgotten in the English-speaking world for two centuries. Now, we shouldn't think of the Puritans as killjoys (as our culture so often portrays them). Their opposition to Christmas was primarily spiritual. The Puritans were staunch Protestants, and they opposed anything that might draw the people back to Roman Catholicism. And Christmas was a big part of the Roman Catholic system. The name Christmas, or Christ-mass, came from the December 25th observance of the Catholic mass, which the Puritans took to be unbiblical. It was just one more holy day in an extensive liturgical calendar, which involved the veneration of saints and other extra-biblical practices. Over the centuries, Christmas celebrations had taken on pagan customs and traditions that had little to do with Christianity. Far from being a family-friendly holiday, Christmas was often marked by debauchery and drunkenness. As a result, during the years when the Puritans were in power, they worked with Parliament to pass laws forbidding shops from closing on Christmas and threatening fines for those caught celebrating. In America, restrictions were not as strong, but Christmas still was not the national event that it is today. Children still went to school on Christmas. Stores remained open. Congress continued to meet. Think of it like Ash Wednesday or Pentecost Sunday for Protestants today; some might observe it, but life and work carried on as normal.

But in the nineteenth century, Christmas took on a new cultural popularity in the English-speaking world, thanks to two main factors. The first was the publication of Charles Dickens's *A Christmas Carol* in 1843. Modern readers may view the classic as a portrayal of Christmas in Dickens's day, which is partly true. But the book was as much an effort to revive Christmas and bring it back into cultural prominence. *A Christmas Carol* became so popular that Dickens went on multiple tours to give sold-out dramatic readings of the book in packed venues throughout America and England. After 1843, Dickens would continue to publish yearly Christmas stories, though none of them matched *A Christmas Carol* in popularity. Interestingly, however, these stories rarely, if ever, mentioned the birth of Christ.

The other factor in reviving Christmas in the nineteenth century was the influence of Prince Albert and Queen Victoria. Prince Albert brought over to England several of his native German Christmas traditions (Christmas had never died out under Lutheranism), and those celebrations were widely publicized. There was one illustration that was especially famous, published in the *Illustrated London News* in December 1848, which pictured Albert and Victoria, their children, and the governess gathered around a Christmas tree with lights and presents. In many ways, this was a portrayal of the Victorian ideal. The royal family not only introduced new traditions to the English (Christmas trees, gifts, candles, etc.), but, more importantly, they made Christmas a family celebration. Rather than Christmas being associated with revelry and drunkenness, it was now centered around the family and the home. The popularity of the holiday continued to expand in this era, fueling the renewed celebration of Christmas as a time for family traditions, holiday meals, and gift-giving.[1]

Amid this intersection of Victorian culture, English Puritanism, and Christmas lived Charles Haddon Spurgeon (1834–1892). Shortly after his conversion, this country boy began to preach at the age of 16, was called to pastor in London at 19, and within 7 years, he was pastoring the largest church in evangelicalism, the Metropolitan Tabernacle. He preached as often as 13 times a week, and millions of his published sermons were sold around the world throughout his 38-year preaching ministry. Through his church, he founded the Pastors' College, two orphanages, and dozens of evangelistic and benevolent institutions, and the impact of his ministry continues to be felt today. Many would consider him the greatest preacher of his generation.

And as a Victorian who read Dickens and admired the royal family, it's no surprise that Spurgeon loved Christmas! Preaching in London in 1855, he declared, "I wish there were ten or a dozen Christmas-days in the

---

1. For a cultural history of Christmas and the revival of Christmas in the nineteenth century, see Bruce David Forbes, *Christmas: A Candid History* (Berkeley: University of California Press, 2007).

year; for there is work enough in the world, and a little more rest would not hurt laboring people. Christmas-day is really a boon to us, particularly as it enables us to assemble round the family hearth and meet our friends once more."[2] He welcomed the holiday season as an opportunity for rest and being reunited with friends and family, especially for his working-class congregation. On Christmas day, he would not only spend time with his family, but he would visit his orphanages and distribute gifts to the children.

At the same time, Spurgeon was an heir of the Puritans. During a time when Roman Catholic theology was experiencing a resurgence in England, Spurgeon championed the evangelical doctrines of the Protestant Reformation. Even as he promoted Christmas, he was careful to ward off any superstition surrounding the holiday.

> We have no superstitious regard for times and seasons. Certainly we do not believe in the present ecclesiastical arrangement called Christmas. First, because we do not believe in the mass at all, but abhor it, whether it be sung in Latin or in English; and secondly, because we find no Scriptural warrant whatever for observing any day as the birthday of the Savior; and consequently, its

2. C. H. Spurgeon, *The New Park Street Pulpit: Containing Sermons Preached and Revised by the Rev. C. H. Spurgeon, Minister of the Chapel.* 6 vols. (London: Passmore & Alabaster, 1855-1860.), 2:25. Henceforth, *NPSP*. This work will also cite C. H. Spurgeon, *The Metropolitan Tabernacle Pulpit: Sermons Preached and Revised by C. H. Spurgeon*, vols. 7–63 (London: Passmore & Alabaster, 1861–1917). Henceforth, *MTP.*

observance is a superstition, because not of divine authority. Superstition has fixed most positively the day of our Savior's birth, although there is no possibility of discovering when it occurred. . . . Probably the fact is that the "holy" days were arranged to fit in with the heathen festivals. We venture to assert, that if there be any day in the year, of which we may be pretty sure that it was not the day on which the Savior was born, it is the twenty-fifth of December.

Spurgeon taught his people not to treat Christmas in any way as "sacred." We see this especially in the gatherings of his church on Christmas Sundays. Unlike other churches, he treated those gatherings just like any other Sunday: no special decorations, no new liturgy. One local newspaper gave this report on Christmas Sunday at the Tabernacle in 1870:

> At the Metropolitan Tabernacle on Sunday there were no outward signs of Christmas. The Tabernacle wore its usual appearance, only that owing probably to the inclemency of the weather it was not as crowded as it ordinarily is, and indeed was not quite full, and the fog was so thick that the gas was lit, Mr. Spurgeon was hardly discernible, except by those who were near the platform. But his voice rang out clear and distinct as ever.[3]

For the sermons he preached on Christmas Sundays, Spurgeon didn't mind preaching on Christmas texts,

---

3. "Christmas Day at the Metropolitan Tabernacle," *South London Press*, December 31, 1870, 10, The British Newspaper Archive.

like Isaiah 9:6,[4] Micah 5:2,[5] or Luke 2:7.[6] As he once said, "Although we do not fall exactly in the track of other people, I see no harm in thinking of the incarnation and birth of the Lord Jesus."[7] Even so, he didn't always preach on a Christmas theme. Some years, he simply carried on with his normal preaching habit, which was to preach on a Scripture text given to him by the Spirit in prayer. And so, on any given Christmas, his congregation might hear him preach on the infallibility of Scripture from Matthew 4:4[8] or on repentance from Jeremiah 18:11.[9] Also, Spurgeon did not limit his preaching on the birth of Christ only to December. Rather, throughout the year, he regularly taught about the incarnation and preached from Nativity texts. On those Sundays, the congregation enjoyed hearing a Scripture reading about the birth of Christ and singing Christmas carols in the middle of the year.[10] The incarnation was a wonder to be marveled at all year round.

---

4. "A Christmas Question," preached on Dec. 25, 1859, *NPSP*, vol. 6, sermon 291.

5. "The Incarnation and Birth of Christ," preached on Dec. 23, 1855, *NPSP*, vol. 2, sermon 57.

6. "No Room for Christ in the Inn," preached on Dec. 21, 1862, *MTP*, vol. 8, sermon 485.

7. "The Incarnation and Birth of Christ," preached on Dec. 23, 1855, *NPSP* 2:25.

8. "Infallibility – Where to Find It and How to Use It," preached on Dec. 20, 1874, *MTP*, vol. 20, sermon 1208.

9. "Return! Return!", preached on Dec. 21, 1884, *MTP*, vol. 43, sermon 2547.

10. For example, see "The True Tabernacle, and Its Glory of Grace and Peace," preached on September 27, 1885, *MTP*, vol. 31, sermon 1862. One of the hymns sung in this service was Hymn 256 from the church's hymnal, "Hark, the Herald Angels Sing."

Even as Christmas grew into a cultural phenomenon, Spurgeon lived during a time when the doctrine of the incarnation was being challenged. With the growth of German higher criticism, the authority and trustworthiness of Scripture were increasingly being challenged. The translation of David Strauss's *The Life of Jesus* into English in 1846 led many to adopt a rationalistic understanding of the Gospels, stripping them of all supernatural elements. For them, the incarnation was no longer the miraculous joining of the eternal Son of God with our humanity. Rather, it was simply mythical language that pointed to the high view the disciples had of their rabbi. As evangelicals encountered this teaching, many responded by shifting their emphasis from salvation to ethics. After all, morality was something both conservatives and progressives could agree on. For some, this meant shifting their teaching away from Jesus's death and resurrection to the incarnation. This allowed them to focus more on God's immanence (as opposed to his transcendence) and Jesus's love and moral teaching, and downplay any mention of sin, judgment, or salvation.

Spurgeon would have none of this. Throughout his ministry, and especially during Christmas, he took every opportunity to proclaim the gospel: that the Son of God became a man in order that he might be the perfect sacrifice for the salvation of sinners. The incarnation is not a myth. It is a theological wonder on which our hope depends. The miracle of the virgin birth, the appearance of the angels, God's orchestrating of history, and every other supernatural element of the Nativity pointed to the fact that something wonderful had taken place: "The Infinite has become an infant; he, upon whose shoulders the universe hangs, hangs at his mother's breast; he who created all things, and bears up the pillars of creation, has now become so weak, that he must be carried by a woman!"[11] And yet, this incarnation did not happen so that Christ could be for us merely a moral example. Rather, he came first and foremost to be our Savior. The wonder of Christmas is that the God against whom we have sinned would ever send us such a gracious gift. And yet, this is what he did in the little town of Bethlehem many years ago:

> Though it is eighteen hundred years ago and more, the Christmas bells seem to ring on. The joy of his coming is still in our hearts. He lived here his two or three and thirty years, but he was sent, the text tells us, for a reason which caused him to die. He was sent for sin. . . . He was sent that he might be the substitute for sinners. God's great plan was this, that inasmuch as his justice could not overlook sin, and sin must be punished, Jesus Christ should come and take the sin of his people upon himself, and upon the accursed tree, the cross of ignominious note, should suffer what was due on our behalf, and that then through his sufferings the infinite love of God should stream forth without any contravention of his infinite justice. This is what God did. He sent his Son to Bethlehem; he sent his Son to Calvary.[12]

---

11. *NPSP* 3:351.
12. *MTP* 16:291-292.

How can Christians properly celebrate Christmas? Certainly, Christmas trees, gift-giving, family reunions, and many other customs can all be joyful traditions of the season. But Spurgeon would say that the primary way to celebrate Christmas is by faith in the incarnate, crucified, and risen Savior. That's why this devotional exists: amid a busy holiday season, it is meant to be a daily help to us, reminding us why we celebrate.

The readings in this volume are taken from Spurgeon's sermons and are designed to help you grow a deeper understanding of the theology of Christmas and a greater love for the Savior. They have been lightly edited for a modern audience. I've also added verse references to help you refer back to the Scriptures. They're not organized according to any liturgical calendar (which I think Spurgeon would have appreciated!). You can certainly read them during the Advent season (which begins four Sundays before Christmas), but these readings would be edifying anytime throughout the year. More importantly, however you read this devotional, treasure these truths and ponder them in your heart. Only as we embrace the Savior by faith can we come to know the true joy of Christmas.

Geoffrey Chang
Kansas City, MO
October 26, 2023

Day 1

Christ, the Conqueror of Satan

"I will put enmity between you and the woman,
and between your offspring and her offspring;
he shall bruise your head,
and you shall bruise his heel."
Genesis 3:15

This is the first gospel sermon that was ever delivered upon the surface of this earth. It was a memorable discourse indeed, with Jehovah himself for the preacher, and the whole human race and the prince of darkness for the audience. It must be worthy of our heartiest attention.

Is it not remarkable that this great gospel promise should have been delivered so soon after the transgression? As yet no sentence had been pronounced upon either of the two human offenders, but the promise was given under the form of a sentence pronounced upon the serpent. Not yet had the woman been condemned to painful travail, or the man to exhausting labor, or even the soil to the curse of thorn and thistle. Truly "mercy triumphs over judgment" (James 2:13). Before the Lord had said "You are dust, and to dust you shall return," he was pleased to say that the seed of the woman should bruise the serpent's head (Genesis 3:19). Let us rejoice, then, in the swift mercy of God, which in the early watches of the night of sin came with comfortable words unto us.

The seed of the woman by promise is to champion the cause, and oppose the dragon. That seed is the Lord Jesus Christ. The prophet Micah says,

> But you, O Bethlehem Ephrathah, who are too little to be among the clans of Judah, from you shall come forth for me one who is to be ruler in Israel, whose coming forth is from of old, from ancient days. Therefore he shall give them up until the time when she who is in labor has given birth. (Micah 5:2–3)

To none other than the babe which was born in Bethlehem of the blessed Virgin can the words of prophecy refer. She it was who did conceive and bear a son, and it is concerning her son that we sing,

> For to us a child is born, to us a son is given; and the government shall be upon his shoulder, and his name shall be called Wonderful Counselor, Mighty God, Everlasting Father, Prince of Peace. (Isaiah 9:6)

On the memorable night at Bethlehem, when angels sang in heaven, the seed of the woman appeared, and as soon as ever he saw the light the old serpent, the devil, entered into the heart of Herod if possible to slay him, but the Father preserved him, and suffered none to lay hands on him. As soon as he publicly came forward upon the stage of action, thirty years after, Satan met him foot to foot. You know the story of the temptation in the wilderness, and how there the woman's seed fought with him who was a liar from the beginning.

The devil assailed him thrice with all the artillery of flattery, malice, craft, and falsehood, but the peerless champion stood unwounded, and chased his foeman from the field. Then our Lord set up his kingdom, and called one and another unto him, and carried the war into the enemy's country. In various places he cast out devils. He spoke to the wicked and unclean spirit and said, "I command you, come out of him" (Mark 9:25), and the demon was expelled. Legions of devils flew before him: they sought to hide themselves in swine to escape from the terror of his presence. "Have you come here to torment us before the time?"(Matthew 8:29) was their cry when the wonder-working Christ dislodged them from the bodies which they tormented. Yea, and he made his own disciples mighty against the evil one, for in his name they cast out devils, till Jesus said, "I saw Satan fall like lightning from heaven" (Luke 10:18). Then there came a second personal conflict, for I take it that Gethsemane's sorrows were to a great degree caused by a personal assault of Satan, for our Master said, "This is your hour, and the power of darkness" (Luke 22:53). He said also, "The ruler of this world is coming" (John 14:30). What a struggle it was. Though Satan had nothing in Christ, yet did he seek if possible to lead him away from completing his great sacrifice, and there did our Master sweat as it were great drops of blood, falling to the ground, in the agony which it cost him to contend with the fiend (Luke 22:44). Then it was that our Champion began the last fight of all and won it to the bruising of the serpent's head. Nor did he end till he had spoiled principalities and powers and made a show of them openly.

Now is the hour of darkness past,
Christ has assumed his reigning power;
Behold the great accuser cast
Down from his seat to reign no more.

The conflict our glorious Lord continues in his seed. We preach Christ crucified, and every sermon shakes the gates of hell. We bring sinners to Jesus by the Spirit's power, and every convert is a stone torn down from the wall of Satan's mighty castle. Yea, and the day shall come when everywhere the evil one shall be overcome, and the words of John in the Revelation shall be fulfilled. "And the great dragon was thrown down, that ancient serpent, who is called the devil and Satan, the deceiver of the whole world—he was thrown down to the earth, and his angels were thrown down with him. And I heard a loud voice in heaven, saying, 'Now the salvation and the power and the kingdom of our God and the authority of his Christ have come, for the accuser of our brothers has been thrown down, who accuses them day and night before our God'" (Revelation 12:9–10). Thus did the Lord God in the words of our text promise a champion who should be the seed of the woman, between whom and Satan there should be war for ever and ever: that champion has come, the son has been born, and though the dragon is filled with wrath against the woman, and makes war with the remnant of her seed which keep the testimony of Jesus Christ, yet the battle is the Lord's, and the victory falls to him whose name is Faithful and True, who in righteousness judges and makes war.

Day 2
The Prophet Like Moses

"I will raise up for them a prophet like you from among
their brothers. And I will put my words in his mouth,
and he shall speak to them all that I command him."
Deuteronomy 18:18

M an, the creature, may well desire communion with
his Creator. When we are right-minded we cannot
bear to be like fatherless children, born into the world
by a parent of whom we know nothing whatever. We
long to hear our father's voice. Of old time, before sin
had entered the world, the Lord God was on the most
intimate terms with his creature man. He communed
with Adam in the garden; in the cool of the day, he
made the evening to be seven-fold refreshing by the
shadow of his own presence (Genesis 3:8). There was no
cloud between unfallen man and the ever blessed One.
They could commune together, for no sin had set up a
middle wall of partition.

Alas, man, being in honor, continued not, but
broke the law of his God. And he not only forfeited
his own inheritance, but entailed upon his descendants
a character with which the holy God can hold no con-
verse. By nature we love that which is evil, and within
us there is an evil heart of unbelief in departing from
the living God, and consequently communion between
God and man has had to be upon quite another footing
from that which commenced and ended in the glades of
Eden. It was condescension at the first, which made the

Lord speak with man the creature; it is mercy, unutterable mercy, now if God deigns to speak with man the sinner.

Through his divine grace the Lord did not leave our fathers altogether without a word from himself even after the Fall, for between the days of Adam and Moses there were occasional voices heard as of God speaking with man. "Enoch walked with God" (Genesis 5:22), which implies that God walked with him and had communion with him, and we may rest assured it was no silent walk which Enoch had with the Most High. The Lord also spoke to Noah, once and again, and made a covenant with him (Genesis 9:1–17). And then he, at still greater length and with greater frequency, spoke with Abraham, whom he graciously called his friend (James 2:23). Voices also came to Isaac, and Jacob, and Joseph, and celestial beings flitted to and fro between earth and heaven.

Then there was a long pause and a dreary silence. No prophet spoke in Jehovah's name, no voice of God in priestly oracle heard, but all was silent while Israel dwelt in Egypt, and sojourned in the land of Ham. So completely hushed was the spiritual voice among men that it seemed as if God had utterly forsaken his people and left the world without a witness to his name; yet there was a prophecy of his return, and the Lord had great designs, which only waited till the full time was come. He purposed to try man in a very special manner, to see whether he could bear the presence of the Lord or not. He resolved to take a family, multiply it into a nation, and set it apart for himself, and to that nation he would make a revelation of himself of the most extra-ordinary character. So, he took the people who slaved amongst the brick kilns of Egypt, and made them his elect, the nation of his choice, ordained to be a nation of priests, a people near unto him, if they had but grace to bear the honor. Though they had lain among the pots, with a high hand and an outstretched arm he delivered them, and with gracious love he favored them, so that they became for beauty and excellence as the wings of a dove that are covered with silver and her feathers with yellow gold. He divided the Red Sea and made them a way of escape, and afterwards set that sea as a barrier between them and their former masters. He took them into the wilderness, and there fed them with manna which dropped from heaven, and with water out of the rock did he sustain them. After a while he began to speak to them, as he had never spoken to any nation before. He spoke with them from the top of Sinai, so that they heard his voice out of the midst of the fire, and in astonishment they cried, "This day we have seen God speak with man, and man still live" (Deuteronomy 5:24).

But the experiment failed. Man was not in a condition to hear the direct voice of God. On the very first day the people were in such terror and alarm that they cried out, "This great fire will consume us. If we hear the voice of the LORD our God any more, we shall die" (Deuteronomy 5:25). As they stood still at a distance to hear the words of God's perfect law, they were filled with great fear, and so terrible was the sight that even Moses said, "I tremble with fear" (Hebrew 12:21). The people could not endure that which was commanded, and entreated that the word should not be spoken to them anymore. They felt the need of someone to interpose—a mediator, an interpreter, one of a thousand was needed to come between them and God. Even those among them that were the most spiritual, and understood and loved God better than the rest, yet confessed that they could not endure the thunder of his dreadful voice, and their elders and the heads of their tribes came unto Moses and said, "Go near and hear all that the Lord our God will say, and speak to us all that the Lord our God will speak to you, and we will hear and do it" (Deuteronomy 5:27).

The Lord knew that man would always be unable to hear his Maker's voice, and he therefore determined not only to speak by Moses, but, occasionally, to speak by his servants the prophets, raising up here one and there another; and then he determined, as the consummation of his condescending mercy, that at the last he would put all the word he had to say to man into one heart, and that word should be spoken by one mouth to men, furnishing a full, complete, and unchangeable revelation of himself to the human race. This he resolved to give by one of whom Moses had learned something when the Lord said to him in the words of our text, "I will raise up for them a prophet like you from among their brothers. And I will put my words in his mouth, and he shall speak to them all that I command him" (Deuteronomy 18:18). We know assuredly that our Lord Jesus Christ is that prophet like unto Moses by whom in these last days he has spoken unto us. See Peter's testimony in the third chapter of the Acts of the Apostles, and Stephen's in the seventh chapter of the same book. "For Jesus has been counted worthy of more glory than Moses—as much more glory as the builder of a house has more honor than the house itself" (Hebrews 3:3), yet did he bear a gracious likeness to Moses, and therein his apostles found a sure argument of his being indeed the Messiah, sent of God.

Day 3

The True Tabernacle

And the Word became flesh and dwelt among us,
and we have seen his glory, glory as of the only Son
from the Father, full of grace and truth.
John 1:14

If you look attentively at the verse before us, and if you are in some slender measure acquainted with the original languages, you will perceive that John here compares Christ to that which was the greatest glory of the Jewish Church. Let me read it, giving another translation: "The Word was made flesh, and *tabernacled* among us, and we beheld his glory, the glory as of the only begotten of the Father, full of grace and truth."

Now, you remember that in the Jewish Church its greatest glory was that God tabernacled in its midst: not the tent of Moses, not the various pavilions of the prince of the twelve tribes, but the humble tabernacle in which God dwelt, was the boast of Israel. They had the king himself in the midst of them, a present God in their midst. The tabernacle was a tent to which men went when they would commune with God, and it was the spot to which God came manifestly when he would commune with man. To use Matthew Henry's words, it was the "trysting place" between the Creator and the worshipper. Here they met each other through the slaughter of the bullock and the lamb, and there was reconciliation between them twain.

Now, Christ's human flesh was God's tabernacle, and it is in Christ that God meets with man, and in Christ that man has dealings with God. The Jew of old went to God's tent, in the center of the camp, if he would worship; we come to Christ if we would pay our homage. If the Jew would be released from ceremonial uncleanness, after he had performed the rites, he went up to the sanctuary of his God, that he might feel again that there was peace between God and his soul; and we, having been washed in the precious blood of Christ, have access with boldness unto God, even the Father through Christ, who is our tabernacle and the tabernacle of God among men.

Now let us draw the parallel a little further. The greatest glory of the tabernacle itself was the most holy place. In the most holy place, there stood the ark of the covenant, bearing its golden lid called the mercy-seat. Over the mercy-seat stood the cherubim, whose wings met each other, and beneath the wings of the cherubim there was a bright light, known to the Hebrew believer by the name of the Shekinah. That light represented the presence of God. Immediately above that light there might be seen at night a pillar of fire, and by day a spiral column of cloud rose from it, which no doubt expanded itself into one vast cloud, which covered all the camp, and shielded all the Israelites from the blaze of the broiling sun. The glory of the tabernacle, I say, was the Shekinah.

What does our text say? Jesus Christ was God's tabernacle, and "we have seen his glory, glory as of the only Son from the Father." Jesus is not the tabernacle without the glory; he is not as the temple when the voice was heard with the rushing of winds before the siege of Jerusalem (Ezekiel 1:24; 10:1–22), crying, "Arise, let us go hence," (John 14:31 KJV) but he is the temple in which God himself dwelt after a special manner; "For in him the whole fullness of deity dwells bodily" (Colossians 2:9).

The apostle however points to a surpassing excellence in Christ the tabernacle, by which he wondrously excels that of the Jewish Church. "Full of grace and truth." The Jewish tabernacle was rather full of law than full of grace. It is true there were in its rites and ceremonies foreshadowings of grace, but still in repeated sacrifice there was renewed remembrance of sin, and a man had first to be obedient to the law of ceremonies, before he could have access to the tabernacle at all. But Christ is full of grace—not a little of it, but an abundance of it is treasured up in him. The tabernacle of old was not full of truth, but full of image, and shadow, and symbol, and picture. But Christ is full of substance. He is not the picture, but the reality; he is not the shadow, but the substance. Here, O believer, rejoice with joy unspeakable, for you come to Christ, the real tabernacle of God! You come to him who is full of the glory of the Father; and you come to one in whom you have, not the representation of a grace which you need, but the grace itself—not the shadow of a truth ultimately to be revealed, but that very truth by which your soul is accepted in the sight of God. I put this forth as a matter for you to think over in your meditation.

Day 4

The Light after Darkness

> But there will be no gloom for her who was in anguish.
> In the former time he brought into contempt the land
> of Zebulun and the land of Naphtali, but in the latter time
> he has made glorious the way of the sea,
> the land beyond the Jordan, Galilee of the nations.
> The people who walked in darkness
> have seen a great light;
> those who dwelt in a land of deep darkness,
> on them has light shone.
> Isaiah 9:1–2

Further on we find the Lord Jesus as the morning light after a night of darkness. The last verses of the eighth chapter of Isaiah picture a horrible state of wretchedness and despair: "They will pass through the land, greatly distressed and hungry. And when they are hungry, they will be enraged and will speak contemptuously against their king and their God, and turn their faces upward. And they will look to the earth, but behold, distress and darkness, the gloom of anguish. And they will be thrust into thick darkness" (Isaiah 8:21–22).

But see what a change awaits them! Read the fine translation of the Revised Version: "But there will be no gloom for her that was in anguish" (Isaiah 9:1). What a marvelous light from the midst of a dreadful darkness! It is an astounding change, such as only God with us could work. Many of you know nothing about the miseries described in those verses; but there are some here who have traversed that terrible wilderness, and I am going to speak to you. I know where you are this morning: you are being driven as captives into the land of despair, and for the last few months you have been tramping along a painful road, "greatly distressed and hungry." You are sorely put to it, and your soul finds no food of comfort, but is ready to faint and die. You fret yourself; your heart is wearing away with care, and grief, and hopelessness. In the bitterness of your soul you are ready to curse the day of your birth.

The captive Israelites cursed their king who had led them into their defeat and bondage; in the fury of their agony, they even cursed God and longed to die. It may be that your heart is in such a ferment of grief that you know not what you think, but are like a man at his wits' end. Those who led you into sin are bitterly remembered; and as you think upon God you are troubled. This is a dreadful case for a soul to be in, and it involves a world of sin and misery. You look up, but the heavens are as brass above your head; your prayers appear to be shut out from God's ear; you look around you upon the earth, and behold "distress and darkness, the gloom of anguish"; your every hope is slain, and your heart is torn asunder with remorse and dread. Every hour you seem to be hurried by an irresistible power into greater darkness, yea, even into the eternal midnight.

In such a case none can give you comfort save Immanuel, God with us. Only God, espousing your cause, and bearing your sin, can possibly save you. See, he comes for your salvation! Behold, he has come to seek and to save that which was lost. God has come down from heaven, and veiled himself in our flesh, that he might be able to save to the uttermost. He can save the chief of sinners: he can save you. Come to Jesus, you that have gone furthest into transgression, you that sit down in despondency, you that shut yourselves up in the iron cage of despair. For such as you there shines this star of the first magnitude. Jesus has appeared to save, and he is God and man in one person: man, that he may feel our woes, God, that he may help us out of them. No minister can save you, no priest can save you—you know this right well; but here is one who is able to save to the uttermost, for he is God as well as man. The great God is good at a dead lift; whom everything else has failed, the lover of omnipotence can lift a world of sin. Jesus is almighty to save! That which in itself is impossibility is possible with God. Sin which nothing else can remove is blotted out by the blood of Immanuel. Immanuel, our Savior, is God with us; and God with us means difficulty removed, and a perfect work accomplished. But I fail to tell you in words. Oh, that the light itself would shine into your souls, that those of you who have as yet no hope may see a great light, and may from henceforth be of good courage!

Once more, dear friends, we learn from that which follows our text, that the reign of Jesus is the star of the golden future. He came to Galilee of the nations, and made that country glorious, which had been brought into contempt. That corner of Palestine had very often borne the brunt of invasion, and had felt more than any other region the edge of the keen Assyrian sword. They were at first troubled whom the Assyrian was bought off with a thousand talents of silver; but they were more heavily afflicted whom Tiglath-pileser carried them all away to Assyria (2 Kings 15:29). It was a wretched land, with a mixed population, despised by the purer race of Jews; but that very country became glorious with the presence of the incarnate God. It was there that all manner of diseases were healed; there the seas were stilled, and the multitudes were fed; it was there that the Lord Jesus found his apostles, and there he met the whole company of his followers whom he had risen from the dead. That first land to be invaded by the enemy was made the headquarters of the army of salvation: this very Zebulun and Naphtali, which had been so downtrodden and despised, was made the scene of the mighty works of the Son of God. Even so, at this day his gracious presence is the day-dawn of our joy.

Day 5

Jesus of Bethlehem

But you, O Bethlehem Ephrathah,
who are too little to be among the clans of Judah,
from you shall come forth for me
one who is to be ruler in Israel,
whose coming forth is from of old,
from ancient days.

Micah 5:2

The word "Bethlehem" has a double meaning. It signifies "the house of bread," and "the house of war." Ought not Jesus Christ to be born in "the house of bread?" He is the Bread of his people, on which they feed. As our fathers ate manna in the wilderness, so do we live on Jesus here below. Famished by the world, we cannot feed on its shadows. Its husks may gratify the swinish taste of worldlings, for they are swine, but we need something more substantial, and in that blessed bread of heaven, made of the bruised body of our Lord Jesus, and baked in the furnace of his agonies, we find a blessed food. No food like Jesus to the desponding soul or to the strongest saint. The very meanest of the family of God goes to Bethlehem for his bread; and the strongest man, who eats strong meat, goes to Bethlehem for it. House of Bread! Whence could come our nourishment but from you? We have tried Sinai, but on her rugged steeps there grow no fruits, and her thorny heights yield no corn whereon we may feed. We have repaired even to Tabor itself, where Christ was transfigured, and yet there we have not been able to eat his flesh and drink his blood. But Bethlehem, house of bread, rightly you were called, for there the bread of life was first handed down for man to eat.

And it is also called "the house of war," because Christ is to a man either "the house of bread," or "the house of war." While he is food to the righteous, he causes war to the wicked, according to his own word— "Do not think that I have come to bring peace to the earth. I have not come to bring peace, but a sword. For I have come to set a man against his father, and a daughter against her mother, and a daughter-in-law against her mother-in-law. And a person's enemies will be those of his own household" (Matthew 10:34–36). Sinner! if you do not know Bethlehem as "the house of bread," it shall be to you a "house of war." If from the lips of Jesus you never drink sweet honey—if you are not like the bee, which drinks sweet luscious nectar from the Rose of Sharon, then out of the selfsame place there shall go forth against you a two-edged sword; and that mouth from which the righteous draw their bread, shall be to you the mouth of destruction and the cause of your ill.

Jesus of Bethlehem, house of bread and house of war, we trust we know you as our bread. Oh! that some who are now at war with you might hear in their hearts, as well as in their ears the song—

Peace on earth, and mercy mild,
God and sinners reconciled.

And now for that word "Ephrathah." That was the old name of the place which the Jews retained and loved. The meaning of it is "fruitfulness," or "abundance." Ah! well was Jesus born in the house of fruitfulness; Where does my fruitfulness and your fruitfulness come, my brother, but from Bethlehem? Our poor barren hearts never produced one fruit or flower, till they were watered with the Savior's blood. It is his incarnation which fattens the soil of our hearts. There had been pricking thorns on all the ground, and mortal poisons, before he came; but our fruitfulness comes from him. "I am like an evergreen cypress; from me comes your fruit" (Hosea 14:8). "All my springs are in you" (Psalm 87:7). If we be like trees planted by the rivers of water, bringing forth our fruit in our season (Psalm 1:3), it is not because we were naturally fruitful, but because of the rivers of water by which we were planted. It is Jesus that makes us fruitful: "Whoever abides in me," he says, "and I in him, he it is that bears much fruit" (John 15:5). Glorious Bethlehem Ephrathah! Rightly named! Fruitful house of bread—the house of abundant provision for the people of God!

We notice, next, the position of Bethlehem. It is said to be "too little to be among the clans of Judah." Why is this? Because Jesus Christ always goes among little ones. He was born in the little one "among the clans of Judah." Not Bashan's high hill, not on Hebron's royal mount, not in Jerusalem's palaces; but in the humble, yet illustrious, village of Bethlehem. There is a passage in Zechariah which teaches us a lesson: It is said that the man on the red horse stood among the myrtle-trees (Zechariah 1:8). Now the myrtle-trees grow at the bottom of the hill; and the man on the red horse always rides there. He does not ride on the mountain-top; he rides among the humble in heart. "This is the one to whom I will look: he who is humble and contrite in spirit and trembles at my word" (Isaiah 66:2).

There are some little ones here this morning—"little among the clans of Judah." No one ever heard your name, did they? If you were buried, and had your name on your tombstone, it would never be noticed. Those who pass by would say, "It is nothing to me; I never knew him." You do not know much of yourself, or think much of yourself; you can scarcely read, perhaps. Or if you have some talents and ability, you are despised amongst men; or, if you are not despised by them, you despise yourself. You are one of the little ones. Well, Christ is always born in Bethlehem among the little ones. Big hearts never get Christ inside of them; Christ lies not in great hearts, but in little ones. Mighty and proud spirits never have Jesus Christ, for he comes in at low doors, but he will not come in at high ones. He who has a broken heart, and a low spirit, shall have the Savior, but none else. He heals not the prince and the king, but "he heals the brokenhearted and binds up their wounds" (Psalm 147:3). Sweet thought! He is the Christ of the little ones.

Day 6

The People's Christ

"I have exalted one chosen from the people."
Psalm 89:19

Our Savior Jesus Christ, I say, was chosen out of the people; but this merely respects his manhood. As "very God of very God" he was not chosen out of the people; for there was none save him. He was his Father's only-begotten Son, "begotten of the Father before all worlds."[13] He was God's fellow, co-equal, and co-eternal. Consequently, when we speak of Jesus as being chosen out of the people, we must speak of him as a man. We are, I conceive, too forgetful of the real manhood of our Redeemer, for a man he was to all intents and purposes, and I love to sing,

> A Man there was, a real Man,
> Who once on Calvary died

He was not man and God amalgamated—the two natures suffered no confusion—he was very God, without the diminution of his essence or attributes; and he was equally, verily, and truly, man.[14] It is as a man I speak of Jesus this morning; and it rejoices my heart when I can view the human side of that glorious miracle of incarnation, and can deal with Jesus Christ as my brother—inhabitant of the same mortality, wrestler

---

13. Taken from the Nicene Creed
14. Taken from the Chalcedonian Definition

with the same pains and ills, companion in the march of life, and, for a little while, a fellow-sleeper in the cold chamber of death.

We have had many complaints this week, and for some weeks past, in the newspapers, concerning the upper-class families. We are governed—and, according to the firm belief of a great many of us, very badly governed—by certain aristocratic families. We are not governed by men chosen out of the people, as we ought to be; and this is a fundamental wrong in our government—that our rulers, even when elected by us, can scarcely ever be elected from us. Families, where certainly there is not a monopoly of intelligence or prudence, seems to have a patent for promotion; while a man, a commoner, a tradesman, of however good sense, cannot rise to the government. I am no politician, and I am about to preach no political sermon; but I must express my sympathy with the people, and my joy that we, as Christians, are governed by "one chosen from the people." Jesus Christ is the people's man; he is the people's friend—aye, one of themselves. Though he sits high on his Father's throne, he was "one chosen from the people." Christ is not to be called the aristocrat's Christ, he is not the noble's Christ, he is not the king's Christ; but he is "one chosen from the people." It is this thought which cheers the hearts of the people, and ought to bind their souls in unity to Christ, and the holy faith of which he is the Founder and Perfecter (Hebrews 12:2).

Christ, by his very birth, was one of the people. True, he was born of a royal ancestry. Mary and Joseph were both of them descendants of a kingly race, but the glory had departed. A stranger sat on the throne of Judah, while the lawful heir grasped the hammer and the plane. Mark well the place of his nativity. Born in a stable—cradled in a manger where the horned oxen fed—his only bed was their fodder, and his slumbers were often broken by their lowings. He might be a prince by birth; but certainly he had not a princely retinue to wait upon him. He was not clad in purple garments, neither wrapped in embroidered clothing; the halls of kings were not trodden by his feet, the marble palaces of monarchs were not honored by his infant smiles.

Take notice of the visitors who came around his cradle. The shepherds came first of all. We never find that they lost their way. No, God guides the shepherds, and he did direct the wise men too, but they lost their way. It often happens, that while shepherds find Christ, wise men miss him. But, however, both of them came, the magi and the shepherds; both knelt round that manger, to show us that Christ was the Christ of all men; that he was not merely the Christ of the magi, but that he was the Christ of the shepherds—that he was not merely the Savior of the peasant shepherd, but also the Savior of the learned, for

> None are excluded hence, but those
> Who do themselves exclude;
> Welcome the learned and polite,
> The ignorant and rude.

Christ was chosen out of the people—that he might know our wants and sympathize with us. You know the old tale, that one half the world does not know how the other half lives, and that is very true. I believe some of the rich have no notion whatever of what the distress of the poor is. They have no idea of what it is to labor for their daily food. They have a very faint conception of what a rise in the price of bread means. They do not know anything about it; and when we put men in power who never were of the people, they do not understand the art of governing us. But our great and glorious Jesus Christ is one chosen out of the people, and therefore he knows our wants.

My brother Christian, there is no place where you can go, where Christ has not been before, sinful places alone excepted. In the dark valley of the shadow of death you may see his bloody footsteps—footprints marked with gore; ay, and even at the deep waters of the swelling Jordan, you will, when you come hard by the side, say "There are the footprints of a man: whose are they?" Stooping down, you will discern a nail-mark, and will say "Those are the footsteps of the blessed Jesus." He has been before you; he has smoothed the way; he has entered the grave, that he might make the tomb the royal bedchamber of the ransomed race, the closet where they lay aside the garments of labor, to put on the vestments of eternal rest. In all places wherever we go, the angel of the covenant has been our forerunner. Each burden we have to carry, has once been laid on the shoulders of Immanuel.

Day 7

God with Us

"Behold, the virgin shall conceive and bear a son,
and they shall call his name Immanuel"
(which means, God with us).
Matthew 1:23

Never let us for a moment hesitate as to the Godhead of our Lord Jesus Christ, for his Deity is a fundamental doctrine of the Christian faith. It may be that we shall never understand fully how God and man could unite in one person, for who can by searching find out God? These great mysteries of godliness, these "deep things of God" (1 Corinthians 2:10 KJV), are beyond our measurement: our little skiff might be lost if we ventured so far out upon this vast, this infinite ocean, as to lose sight of the shore of plainly revealed truth. But let it remain as a matter of faith that Jesus Christ, even he who lay in Bethlehem's manger, and was carried in a woman's arms, and lived a suffering life and died on a malefactor's cross, was, nevertheless, "God over all, blessed forever" (Romans 9:5), "uphold[ing] the universe by the word of his power" (Hebrews 1:3). He was not an angel—that the apostle has abundantly disproved in the first and second chapters of the epistle to the Hebrews: he could not have been an angel, for honors are ascribed to him which were never bestowed on angels. He was no subordinate deity or being elevated to the Godhead, as some have absurdly said—all these things are dreams and falsehoods; he was as surely God as God can be, one with the Father and the ever-blessed Spirit. If it were not so, not only would the great strength of our hope be gone, but as to this text the sweetness would be evaporated altogether. The very essence and glory of the incarnation is that he was God who was veiled in human flesh: if it was any other being who thus came to us in human flesh, I see nothing very remarkable in it, nothing comforting, certainly. That an angel should become a man is a matter of no great consequence to me: that some other superior being should assume the nature of man brings no joy to my heart, and opens no well of consolation to me.

But "God with us" is exquisite delight. "GOD with us": all that "God" means, the Deity, the infinite Jehovah with us; this, this is worthy of the burst of midnight song, when angels startled the shepherds with their carols, singing "Glory to God in the highest, and on earth peace among those with whom he is pleased" (Luke 2:14). This was worthy of the foresight of seers and prophets, worthy of a new star in the heavens, worthy of the care which inspiration has manifested to preserve the record. This, too, was worthy of the martyr deaths of apostles and confessors who counted not their lives dear unto them for the sake of the incarnate God; and this, my brothers and sisters, is worthy at this day of your most earnest endeavors to spread the glad tidings, worthy of a holy life to illustrate its blessed influences, and worthy of a joyful death to prove its consoling power. Here is the first truth of our holy faith—"Great indeed, we confess, is the mystery of godliness: He was manifested in the flesh" (1 Timothy 3:16).

He who was born at Bethlehem is God, and "God with us." God—there lies the majesty; "God with us," there lies the mercy. God—therein is glory; "God with us," therein is grace. God alone might well strike us with terror; but "God with us" inspires us with hope and confidence.

Let us admire this truth: "God with us." Let us stand at a reverent distance from it as Moses when he saw God in the bush stood a little back, and put his shoes from off his feet, feeling that the place on which he stood was holy ground. This is a wonderful fact, God the Infinite once dwelt in the frail body of a child, and tabernacled in the suffering form of a lowly man. "God was in Christ" (2 Corinthians 5:19 KJV). "He made himself of no reputation, and took upon him the form of a servant, and was made in the likeness of men" (Philippians 2:7 KJV).

Observe the wonder of condescension contained in this fact, that God who made all things should assume the nature of one of his own creatures, that the self-existent should be united with the dependent and derived, and the Almighty linked with the feeble and mortal. In the case before us, the Lord descended to the very depth of humiliation, and entered into alliance with a nature which did not occupy the chief place in the scale of existence. It would have been great conde-scension for the infinite and incomprehensible Jehovah to have taken upon himself the nature of some noble spiritual being, such as a seraph or a cherub. The union of the divine with a created spirit would have been an unmeasurable stoop, but for God to be one with man is far more.

Remember that in the person of Christ manhood was not merely quickening spirit, but also suffering, hungering, dying, flesh and blood. There was taken to himself by our Lord all that materialism which makes up a body, and a body is after all but the dust of the earth, a structure fashioned from the materials around us. There is nothing in our bodily frame but what is to be found in the substance of the earth on which we live. We feed upon that which grows out of the earth, and when we die we go back to the dust from where we were taken. Is not this a strange thing that this grosser part of creation, this meaner part, this dust of it, should nevertheless be taken into union, with that pure, marvelous, incomprehensible, divine being of whom we know so little, and can comprehend nothing at all? Oh, the condescension of it! I leave it to the meditations of your quiet moments. Dwell on it with awe. I am persuaded that no man has any idea how wonderful a stoop it was for God thus to dwell in human flesh, and to be "God with us."

Yet, to make it appear still more remarkable, remember that the creature whose nature Christ took was a being that had sinned. I can more readily conceive the Lord's taking upon himself the nature of a race which had never fallen; but, lo, the race of man stood in rebellion against God, and yet a man did Christ become, that he might deliver us from the consequences of our rebellion, and lift us up to something higher than our pristine purity. "God sending his own Son in the likeness of sinful flesh, and for sin, condemned sin in the flesh" (Romans 8:3 KJV). "Oh, the depth" (Romans 11:33), is all that we can say, as we look on and marvel at this stoop of divine love.

Day 8

Mary's Song

And Mary said,
"My soul magnifies the Lord,
and my spirit rejoices in God my Savior."
Luke 1:46–47

Observe, that Mary sings. Her subject is a Savior; she hails the incarnate God. The long-expected Messiah is about to appear. He for whom prophets and princes waited long, is now about to come, to be born of the virgin of Nazareth. Truly there was never a subject of sweeter song than this—the stooping down of Godhead to the feebleness of manhood. When God manifested his power in the works of his hands, the morning stars sang together, and the sons of God shouted for joy; but when God manifests himself what music shall suffice for the grand psalm of adoring wonder? When wisdom and power are seen, these are but attributes; but in the incarnation it is the divine person which is revealed wrapped in a veil of our inferior clay.

Well might Mary sing, when earth and heaven even now are wondering at the condescending grace! Worthy of peerless music is the fact that "the Word became flesh and dwelt among us" (John 1:14). There is no longer a great gulf fixed between God and his people; the humanity of Christ has bridged it over. We can no more think that God sits on high, indifferent to the wants and woes of men, for God has visited us and come down to the lowliness of our estate. No longer need we bemoan that we can never participate in the moral glory and purity of God, for if God in glory can come down to his sinful creature, it is certainly less difficult to bear that creature, blood-washed and purified, up that starry way, that the redeemed one may sit down for ever on his throne. Let us dream no longer in somber sadness that we cannot draw near to God so that he will really hear our prayer and pity our necessities, seeing that Jesus has become bone of our bone and flesh of our flesh, born a babe as we are born, living a man as we must live, bearing the same infirmities and sorrows, and bowing his head to the same death. O, can we not come with boldness by this new and living way, and have access to the throne of the heavenly grace (Hebrews 10:19–20), when Jesus meets us as Immanuel, God with us?

Angels sung, but they scarce knew why. Could they understand why God had become man? They must have known that here was a mystery of condescension. But all the loving consequences which the incarnation involved even their acute minds could scarce have guessed. But we see the whole and comprehend the grand design most fully. The manger of Bethlehem was big with glory. In the incarnation was wrapped up all the blessedness by which a soul, snatched from the depths of sin, is lifted up to the heights of glory. Shall not our clearer knowledge lead us to heights of song which angelic guesses could not reach? Shall the lips of cherubs move to flaming sonnets, and shall we who are redeemed by the blood of the incarnate God be treacherously and ungratefully silent!

Did archangels sing thy coming?
Did the shepherds learn their lays?—
Shame would cover me ungrateful,
Should my tongues refuse to praise.

This, however, was not the full subject of her holy hymn. Her peculiar delight was not that there was a Savior to be born, but that he was to be born of her. Blessed among women was she, and highly favored of the Lord. But we can enjoy the same favor; nay, we *must* enjoy it, or the coming of a Savior will be of no avail to us! Christ on Calvary, I know, takes away the sin of his people, but none have ever known the virtue of Christ upon the cross, unless they have the Lord Jesus formed in them as the hope of glory. The stress of the virgin's song is laid upon God's special grace to her. Those little words, the personal pronouns, tell us that it was truly a personal affair with her. "My soul magnifies the Lord, and my spirit rejoices in God my Savior." The Savior was peculiarly, and in a special sense, hers. She sung no "Christ for all." "Christ for me," was her glad subject.

Beloved, is Christ Jesus in your heart? Once you looked at him from a distance, and that look cured you of all spiritual diseases, but are you now living upon him, receiving him into your very vitals as your spiritual meat and drink? In holy fellowship you have oftentimes fed upon his flesh and been made to drink of his blood. You have been buried with him in baptism unto death. You have yielded yourselves a sacrifice to him and you have taken him to be a sacrifice for you. You can sing of him as the spouse did, "His left hand is under my head, and his right hand embraces me! . . . My beloved is mine, and I am his; he grazes among the lilies" (Song of Solomon 2:6, 16).

This is a happy style of living, and all short of this poor slavish work. Oh! you can never know the joy of Mary unless Christ becomes truly and really yours. But oh! when he is yours, yours within, reigning in your heart, yours controlling all your passions, yours changing your nature, subduing your corruptions, inspiring you with hallowed emotions; yours within, a joy unspeakable and full of glory—oh! then you can sing, you must sing, who can restrain your tongue? If all the scoffers and mockers upon earth should bid you hold your peace, you must sing; for your spirit must rejoice in God your Savior.

Day 9
The Riches of Christ

Have this mind among yourselves, which is yours
in Christ Jesus, who, though he was in the form of God,
did not count equality with God a thing to be grasped,
but emptied himself, by taking the form of a servant,
being born in the likeness of men.
Philippians 2:5-7

Now, in the past eternity which had elapsed before his mission to this world, we are told that Jesus Christ was rich; and to those of us who believe his glories and trust in his divinity, it is not hard to see how he was so. Jesus was rich in possessions. Lift up your eyes believer, and for a moment review the riches of my Lord Jesus, before he condescended to become poor for you.

Behold him, sitting upon his throne and declaring his own all-sufficiency. "If I were hungry, I would not tell you, for the cattle on a thousand hills are mine. Mine are the hidden treasures of gold; mine are the pearls that the diver cannot reach; mine every precious thing that earth has seen." The Lord Jesus might have said, "I can stretch my scepter from the east even to the west, and all is mine; the whole of this world, and worlds that glitter in far off space, all are mine. The illimitable expanse of unmeasured space, filled as it is with worlds that I have made, all this is mine. Fly upward, and you cannot reach the summit of the hill of my dominions; dive downward, and you cannot enter into the innermost depths of my sway. From the highest throne in glory to the lowest pit of hell, all, all is mine without exception. I can put the broad arrow of my kingdom upon everything that I have made."

Now, whatever might be the wealth of Christ in things created, he had the power of creation, and therein lay his boundless wealth. If he had pleased he could have spoken worlds into existence; he had but to lift his finger, and a new universe as boundless as the present would have leaped into existence. At the will of his mind, millions of angels would have stood before him, legions of bright spirits would have flashed into being. He spoke, and it was done; he commanded, and it stood fast. He who said, "Light, be," and light was (Genesis 1:3), had power to say to all things, "Be," and they should be. Herein then, lay his riches; this creating power was one of the brightest jewels of his crown.

Our Lord Jesus had honor, honor such as none but a divine being could receive. When he sat upon his throne, before he relinquished the glorious mantle of his sovereignty to become a man, all earth was filled with his glory. He could look both beneath and all around him, and the inscription, "Glory be unto God," was written over all space; day and night the smoking incense of praise ascended before him from golden censers held by spirits who bowed in reverence; the harps of thousands of cherubim and seraphim continually thrilled with his praise, and the voices of all those mighty hosts were ever eloquent in adoration. It may be, that on set days the princes from the far-off realms, the kings, the mighty ones of his boundless realms, came to the court of

Christ, and brought each his annual revenue. Oh, who can tell but that in the vast eternity, at certain grand eras, the great bell was rung, and all the mighty hosts that were created gathered together in solemn review before his throne? Who can tell the high holiday that was kept in the court of heaven when these bright spirits bowed before his throne in joy and gladness, and, all united, raised their voices in shouts and hallelujahs such as mortal ear has never heard? Oh, can you tell the depths of the rivers of praise that flowed hard by the city of God? Can you imagine to yourselves the sweetness of that harmony that perpetually poured into the ear of Jesus, Messiah, King, Eternal, equal with God his Father? No; at the thought of the glory of his kingdom, and the riches and majesty of his power, our souls are spent within us, our words fail, we cannot utter a fraction of his glories.

Nor was he poor in any other sense. Without love, man is poor—give him all the diamonds, and pearls, and gold that mortal has conceived. But Jesus was not poor in love. When he came to earth, he did not come to get our love because his soul was lonely. Oh no, his Father had a full delight in him from all eternity. The heart of Jehovah, the first person of the Sacred Trinity, was divinely, immutably linked to him; he was beloved of the Father and of the Holy Spirit; the three persons took a sacred satisfaction and delight in each other. And besides that, how was he loved by those bright spirits who had not fallen. I cannot tell what countless orders and creatures there are created who still stand fast in obedience to God. It is not possible for us to know whether there are, or not, as many races of created beings as we know there are created men on earth. We cannot tell but that in the boundless regions of space, there are worlds inhabited by beings infinitely superior to us. But certain it is, there were the holy angels, and they loved our Savior. They stood day and night with wings outstretched, waiting for his commands, hearkening to the voice of his word, and when he bade them fly, there was love in their countenance, and joy in their hearts. They loved to serve him, and it is not all fiction that when there was war in heaven, and when God cast out the devil and his legions, then the elect angels showed their love to him, being valiant in fight and strong in power. He wanted not our love to make him happy, he was rich enough in love without us.

Jesus, who is he that could look upon the brow of your Majesty, who is he that could comprehend the strength of the arm of your might? You are God, you are infinite, and we poor finite things, are lost in you. The insect of an hour cannot comprehend you. We bow before you, we adore you; you are God over all, blessed forever. But as for the comprehension of your boundless riches, as for being able to tell your treasures, or to reckon up your wealth, that were impossible. All we know is, that the wealth of God, that the treasures of the infinite, that the riches of eternity, were all your own: you were rich beyond all thought.

Day 10
The Condescension of Christ

For you know the grace of our Lord Jesus Christ,
that though he was rich, yet for your sake he became poor,
so that you by his poverty might become rich.
2 Corinthians 8:9

Oh, how surprised angels were, when they were first informed that Jesus Christ, the Prince of Light and Majesty, intended to shroud himself in clay and become a babe, and live and die! We know not how it was first mentioned to the angels, but when the rumor first began to get afloat among the sacred hosts, you may imagine what strange wonderment there was. What! was it true that he whose crown was all adorned with stars, would lay that crown aside? What! was it certain that he about whose shoulders was cast the purple of the universe, would become a man dressed in a peasants garment? Could it be true that he who was everlasting and immortal, would one day be nailed to a cross? Oh! how their wonderment increased! They desired to look into it.

And when he descended from on high, they followed him; for Jesus was "seen by angels" (1 Timothy 3:16), and seen in a special sense; for they looked upon him in rapturous amazement, wondering what it all could mean. "For your sake he became poor." Do you see him, as on that day of heaven's eclipse he did ungird his majesty? Oh, can you conceive the yet increasing wonder of the heavenly hosts when the deed was actually done, when they saw the tiara taken off, when they saw him unbind his girdle of stars, and cast away his sandals of gold? Can you conceive it, when he said to them, "I do not disdain the womb of the virgin; I am going down to earth to become a man?" Can you picture them as they declared they would follow him! Yes, they followed him as near as the world would permit them. And when they came to earth, they began to sing, "Glory to God in the highest, on earth peace among those with whom he is pleased!" (Luke 2:14). Nor would they go away till they had made the shepherds wonder, and till heaven had hung out new stars in honor of the newborn King.

And now wonder, you angels, the Infinite has become an infant; he, upon whose shoulders the universe hangs, hangs at his mother's breast; he who created all things, and bears up the pillars of creation, has now become so weak, that he must be carried by a woman! And oh, wonder, you that knew him in his riches, while you admire his poverty! Where sleeps the newborn king? Had he the best room in Caesar's palace? Has a cradle of gold been prepared for him, and pillows of down, on which to rest his head? No, where the ox fed, in the dilapidated stable, in the manger, there the Savior lies, swathed in the swaddling bands of the children of poverty!

Nor there does he rest long; on a sudden his mother must carry him to Egypt: he goes there, and becomes a stranger in a strange land. When he comes back, see him that made the worlds handle the hammer and the nails, assisting his father in the trade of a carpenter! Mark him who has put the stars on high and made them glisten in the night; mark him without one star of glory upon his brow—a simple child, as other children. Yet, leave for a while the scenes of his childhood and his earlier life; see him when he becomes a man, and now ye may say, indeed, that for our sakes he did become poor. Never was there a poorer man than Christ; he was the prince of poverty. Christ stood in the lowest vale of poverty. Look at his dress, it is woven from the top throughout, the garment of the poor! As for his food, he oftentimes did hunger and always was dependent upon the charity of others for the relief of his wants! He who scattered the harvest over the broad acres of the world, had not sometimes wherewithal to stay the pangs of hunger. He who dug the springs of the ocean, sat upon a well and said to a Samaritan woman, "Give me a drink" (John 4:7). He rode in no chariot, he walked his weary way, foot sore, o'er the flints of Galilee. He had nowhere to lay his head. He looked upon the fox as it hurried to its burrow, and the fowl as it went to its resting place, and he said, "Foxes have holes, and the birds of the air have nests, but the Son of Man has nowhere to lay his head" (Matthew 8:20).

He who had once been waited on by angels, becomes the servant of servants, takes a towel, girds himself and washes his disciples' feet! He who was once honored with the hallelujahs of ages, is now spit upon and despised! He who was loved by his Father, and had abundance of the wealth of affection, could say, "He who ate my bread has lifted his heel against me" (John 13:18). Oh for words to picture the humiliation of Christ! What leagues of distance between him that sat upon the throne, and him that died upon the cross! Oh, who can tell the mighty chasm between yon heights of glory, and the cross of deepest woe!

Trace him, Christian, he has left you his manger to show you how God came down to man. He has bequeathed you his cross, to show you how man can ascend to God. Follow him, follow him, all his journey through. Follow him along his *via dolorosa*, until at last you meet him among the olives of Gethsemane; see him sweating great drops of blood! Follow him to the pavement of Gabbatha; see him pouring out rivers of gore beneath the cruel whips of Roman soldiers! With weeping eye follow him to the cross of Calvary, see him nailed there! Mark his poverty, so poor, that they have stripped him naked from head to foot and exposed him to the face of the sun! So poor, that when he asked them for water they gave him vinegar to drink! So poor, that his unpillowed head is girt with thorns in death!

Oh, Son of Man, I know not which to admire most, your height of glory, or your depths of misery! Oh, Man, slain for us, shall we not exalt you? God, over all, blessed for ever, shall we not give you the loudest song? "Though he was rich, yet for your sake he became poor."

Day 11

Laid in the Manger

*And she gave birth to her firstborn son and wrapped
him in swaddling cloths and laid him in a manger,
because there was no place for them in the inn.*

Luke 2:7

Why should Christ be laid in the manger? I think
it was intended thus to show forth his humiliation. He came, according to prophecy, to be "despised
and rejected by men, a man of sorrows and acquainted
with grief" (Isaiah 53:3); he had "no form or majesty"
(v. 2); "a root out of dry ground" (v. 2). Would it have
been fitting that the man who was to die naked on the
cross should be robed in purple at his birth? Would it
not have been inappropriate that the Redeemer who
was to be buried in a borrowed tomb should be born
anywhere but in the humblest shed, and housed anywhere but in the most ignoble manner? The manger and
the cross standing at the two extremities of the Savior's
earthly life seem most fit and congruous the one to the
other. He is to wear through life a peasant's garb; he is
to associate with fishermen; the lowly are to be his disciples; the cold mountains are often to be his only bed; he
is to say, "Foxes have holes, and the birds of the air have
nests, but the Son of Man has nowhere to lay his head"
(Matthew 8:20). Nothing, therefore, could be more fitting than that in his season of humiliation, when he laid
aside all his glory, and took upon himself the form of a

servant, and condescended even to the meanest estate, he should be laid in a manger.

By being in a manger he was declared to be the king of the poor. They, doubtless, were at once able to recognize his relationship to them, from the position in which they found him. I believe it excited feelings of the tenderest brotherly kindness in the minds of the shepherds, when the angel said—"And this will be a sign for you: you will find a baby wrapped in swaddling cloths and lying in a manger" (Luke 2:12). In the eyes of the poor, imperial robes excite no affection, but a man in their own garb attracts their confidence. With what tenacity will workingmen cleave to a leader of their own order, believing in him because he knows their toils, sympathizes in their sorrows, and feels an interest in all their concerns. Great commanders have readily won the hearts of their soldiers by sharing their hardships and roughing it as if they belonged to the ranks.

The King of Men who was born in Bethlehem, was not exempted in his infancy from the common calamities of the poor. Nay, his lot was even worse than theirs. I think I hear the shepherds comment on the manger-birth, "Ah!" said one to his fellow, "then he will not be like Herod the tyrant; he will remember the manger and feel for the poor; poor helpless infant, I feel a love for him even now, what miserable accommodation this cold world yields its Savior; it is not a Caesar that is born to-day; he will never trample down our fields with his armies, or slaughter our flocks for his courtiers, he will be the poor man's friend, the people's monarch; according to the words of our shepherd-king, he shall defend the cause of the poor of the people, give deliverance to the children of the needy" (see Psalm 72:4). Surely the shepherds, and such as they—the poor of the earth, perceived at once that here was the people's king; noble in descent, but still as the Lord has called him, "one chosen out of the people" (Psalm 89:19 KJV).

Great Prince of Peace! The manger was your royal cradle! There, you were presented to all nations as Prince of our race, before whose presence there is neither barbarian, Scythian, bond nor free; but thou art Lord of all (Colossians 3:11). Kings, your gold and silver would have been lavished on him if you had known the Lord of Glory (1 Corinthians 2:8), but inasmuch as you knew him not he was declared with demonstration to be a leader and a witness to the people. The things which are not, under him shall bring to nought the things that are, and the things that are despised which God has chosen (1 Corinthians 1:28), shall under his leadership break in pieces the might, and pride, and majesty of human grandeur.

Further, in thus being laid in a manger, he did, as it were, give an invitation to the most humble to come to him. We might tremble to approach a throne, but we cannot fear to approach a manger. Had we seen the Master at first riding in state through the streets of Jerusalem with garments laid in the way, and the palm-branches strewed, and the people crying, "Hosanna!" we might have thought, though even the thought would have been wrong, that he was not approachable. Even there, riding upon a colt the foal of an ass, he was so meek and lowly, that the young children clustered about him with their boyish "Hosanna!" (Matthew 21:7–9).

Never could there be a being more approachable than Christ. No rough guards pushed poor petitioners away; no array of officious friends were allowed to keep off the importunate widow or the man who clamored that his son might be made whole; the hem of his garment was always trailing where sick folk could reach it, and he himself had a hand always ready to touch the disease, an ear to catch the faintest accents of misery, a soul going forth everywhere in rays of mercy, even as the light of the sun streams on every side beyond that orb itself.

By being laid in a manger he proved himself a priest taken from among men, one who has suffered like his brethren, and therefore can sympathize with our weaknesses (Hebrews 4:15). Of him it was said "A friend of tax collectors and sinners" (Matthew 11:19); "this man receives sinners and eats with them" (Luke 15:2). Even as an infant, by being laid in a manger, he was set forth as the sinner's friend. Come to him, you that are weary and heavy-laden! Come to him, you that are broken in spirit, you who are bowed down in soul! Come to him, you that despise yourselves and are despised of others! Come to him, publican and harlot! Come to him, thief and drunkard! In the manger there he lies, unguarded from your touch and unshielded from your gaze. Bow the knee and kiss the Son of God; accept him as your Savior, for he puts himself into that manger that you may approach him.

Day 12
You Will Find a Baby

"And this will be a sign for you: you will find a baby
wrapped in swaddling cloths and lying in a manger."
Luke 2:12

Now, observe, as you look at this infant, that there is not the remotest appearance of temporal power here. Mark the two little puny arms of a little babe that must be carried. Alas, the nations of the earth look for joy in *military power*. By what means can we make a nation of soldiers? The Prussian method is admirable; we must have thousands upon thousands of armed men and big cannon and ironclad vessels to kill and destroy by wholesale. Is it not a nation's pride to be gigantic in arms? What pride flushes the patriot's cheek when he remembers that his nation can murder faster than any other people. Ah, foolish generation, you are groping in the flames of hell to find your heaven, raking amid blood and bones for the foul thing which you call glory. A nation's joy can never lie in the misery of others. Killing is not the path to prosperity; huge armaments are a curse to the nation itself as well as to its neighbors. The joy of a nation is a golden sand over which no stream of blood has ever rippled. It is only found in that river, the streams whereof make glad the city of God. The weakness of submissive gentleness is true power. Jesus establishes his eternal empire not on force but on love. Here, O people, see your hope; the mild peaceful prince, whose glory is his self-sacrifice, is our true benefactor.

But look again, and you shall observe no *pomp* to dazzle you. Is the child wrapped in purple and fine linen? Ah, no. Sleeps he in a cradle of gold? The manger alone is his shelter. No crown is upon the babe's head, neither does a coronet surround the mother's brow. A simple maiden of Galilee and a little child in ordinary swaddling bands, it is all you see. Alas, the nations are dazzled with a vain show. The pomp of empires, the pageants of kings are their delight. How can they admire those gaudy courts, in which too often glorious apparel, decorations, and rank stand, instead of virtue, chastity, and truth. When will the people cease to be children? Must they forever crave for martial music which stimulates to violence, and delight in a lavish expenditure which burdens them with taxation? These make not a nation great or joyous. Bah! How has the bubble burst across the narrow sea. A bubble empire has collapsed. Ten thousand bayonets and millions of gold proved but a sandy foundation for a Babel throne. Vain are the men who look for joy in pomp; it lies in truth and righteousness, in peace and salvation, of which yonder newborn prince in the garments of a peasant child is the true symbol.

Neither was there *wealth* to be seen at Bethlehem. Here in this quiet island, the bulk of men are comfortably seeking to acquire their thousands by commerce and manufactures. We are the sensible people who follow the main chance, and are not to be deluded by ideas of glory; we are making all the money we can, and wondering that other nations waste so much in fight. The main prop and pillar of England's joy is to be found, as some tell us, in the possession of colonies, in the progress of machinery, in steadily increasing our capital. Is not Mammon a smiling deity? But, here, in the cradle of the world's hope at Bethlehem, I see far more of poverty than wealth. I perceive no glitter of gold or shining of silver. I perceive only a poor babe, so poor, so very poor, that he is in a manger laid; and his mother is a carpenter's wife, a woman who wears neither silk nor gem. Not in your gold, O Britons, will ever lie your joy, but in the gospel enjoyed by all classes, the gospel freely preached and joyfully received. Jesus, by raising us to spiritual wealth, redeems us from the chains of Mammon, and in that liberty gives us joy.

And here, too, I see no *superstition*. I know the artist paints angels in the skies, and surrounds the scene with a mysterious light, of which tradition's tongue of falsehood has said that it made midnight as bright as noon. This is fiction merely. There was nothing more there than the stable, the straw the oxen ate, and perhaps the beasts themselves, and the child in the plainest, simplest manner, wrapped as other children are. The cherubs were invisible and of haloes there were none. Around this birth of joy was no sign of superstition. That demon dared not intrude its tricks and posturings into the sublime spectacle. It would have been there as much out of place as a harlequin in the holy of holies. A simple gospel, a plain gospel, as plain as that babe wrapped in the commonest garments, is this day the only hope for men.

I say, then, to you who would know the only true peace and lasting joy, come to the babe of Bethlehem, in after days the Man of Sorrows, the substitutionary sacrifice for sinners. Come, little children, boys and girls, come, for he also was a boy. "The holy child Jesus" (Acts 4:27 KJV) is the children's Savior, and says still, "Let the little children come to me and do not hinder them" (Matthew 19:14). Come, you maidens, you who are still in the morning of your beauty, and, like Mary, rejoice in God your Savior. The virgin bore him on her bosom, so come and bear him in your hearts, saying, "to us a child is born, to us a son is given" (Isaiah 9:6). And you, men in the fullness of your strength, remember how Joseph cared for him, and watched with reverent solicitude his tender years. Be to his cause as a father and a helper. Sanctify your strength to his service. And you women advanced in years, matrons and widows, come like Anna and bless the Lord that you have seen the salvation of Israel, and you gray heads, who like Simeon are ready to depart, come and take the Savior in your arms, adoring him as your Savior and your all. You shepherds, you simple hearted, you who toil for your daily bread, come and adore the Savior. And stand not back, you wise men, you who know by experience and who by meditation peer into deep truth, come, and like the sages of the East bow low before his presence, and make it your honor to pay honor to Christ the Lord. For my own part, the incarnate God is all my hope and trust.

Day 13

His Name Is Jesus

"She will bear a son, and you shall call his name Jesus,
for he will save his people from their sins."
Matthew 1:21

According to the text, the angel brought a message from the Lord, and said, "You shall call his name Jesus." It is a name which, like him who bears it, has come down from heaven. Our Lord has other names of office and relationship, but this is specially and peculiarly his own personal name, and it is the Father who has so named him. Rest assured, therefore, that it is the best name that he could bear.

God would not have given him a name of secondary value, or about which there would be a trace of dishonor. The name is the highest, brightest, and noblest of names; it is the glory of our Lord to be a Savior. To the best that was ever born of woman, God has given the best name that any son of man could bear. JESUS is the most appropriate name that our Lord could receive. Of this we are quite certain, for the Father knew all about him, and could name him well. He knows much more about the Lord Christ than all saints and angels put together, for "no one knows the Son except the Father" (Matthew 11:27). To perfection the Father knew him, and he names him Jesus. We may be sure, then, that our Lord is most of all a Savior, and is best described by that term. God, the Father, who knows him best, sees this to be his grand characteristic, that he is a Savior, and is best represented by the name "Jesus."

Since infinite wisdom has selected it, we may be sure that it is a name which must be true and must be verified by facts of no mean order. God, who cannot be under a mistake, calls him Jesus, a Savior, and therefore Jesus, a Savior, he must be upon a grand scale, continually, abundantly, and in a most apparent manner. Neither will God refuse to accept the work which he has done, since by the gift of that name he has commissioned him to save sinners. When we plead the name of Jesus before God, we bring him back his own word, and appeal to him by his own act and deed. Is not the name of Jesus to be viewed with reverential delight by each one of us, when we remember where it came from? He is not a Savior of our own setting up! But God the everlasting Father has set him forth for our Deliverer and Savior, saying, "You shall call his name Jesus."

It is a name which the Holy Ghost explains, for he tells us the reason for the name of Jesus—"For he will save his people from their sins." "Savior" is the meaning of the name, but it has a fuller sense hidden within, for in its Hebrew form it means "the salvation of the Lord," or "the Lord of salvation," or "the Savior." The angel interprets it, "he will save," and the word for "he" is very emphatic. According to many scholars, the divine name, the incommunicable title of the Most High is contained in "Joshua," the Hebrew form of Jesus, so that, in full, the word means "Jehovah Savior," and in brief it signifies "Savior." It is given to our Lord because "he saves"—not according to any temporary and common salvation, from enemies and troubles, but he saves from spiritual enemies, and especially from sins. Joshua of old was a savior, Gideon was a savior, David was a savior; but the title is given to our Lord above all others because he is a Savior in a sense in which no one else is or can be—he saves his people from their sins.

The Jews were looking for a Savior; they expected one who would break the Roman yoke and save them from being under bondage to a foreign power, but our divine Lord came not for such a purpose. He came to be a Savior of a more spiritual sort, and to break quite another yoke, by saving his people from their sins. The word "save" is very rich in meaning, its full and exact force can hardly be given in English words. Jesus is salvation in the sense of deliverance and also in that of preservation. He gives health, he is all that is salutary to his people; in the fullest and broadest sense he saves his people. The original word means to preserve, to keep, to protect from danger, and to secure. The grandest meanings generally dwell in the shortest words, and in this case the word "save" is a well where the plummet is long in finding a bottom. Jesus brings a great salvation, or as Paul says "such a great salvation" (Hebrews 2:3) as if he felt that he could never estimate its greatness; he also speaks of it as "eternal salvation" (Hebrews 5:9), even as Isaiah said, "Israel is saved by the LORD with everlasting salvation" (Isaiah 45:17). Glorious beyond measure is the name "Jesus" as it is divinely expounded to us, for by that very exposition the eternal God guarantees the success of the Savior: he declares that he shall save his people, and save his people he must. God himself sets him forth to us as—

Jesus, Savior, Son of God,
Bearer of the sinner's load.

Thus we have a name, dear friends, which we have not even to explain for ourselves. As we did not choose it, so we are not left to expound it. God who gave the text has preached us the sermon. He who appointed the name has given us the reason for it, so that we are not left in ignorance or uncertainty. We might have said, "Yes, his name is Jesus, but it refers to a salvation which was wrought in the olden ages"; but no, the word of the Lord tells us "You shall call his name Jesus, for he will save his people from their sins"; and this is for all time, since he always has a people, and these people evermore need to be saved from their sins. Let us be glad that we have such a Savior, and that the name of Jesus retains all the sweetness and power it ever had, and shall retain it till all the chosen people are saved, and then for ever and ever.

Day 14

The Sages,
the Star, and the Savior

"Where is he who has been born king of the Jews? For we
saw his star when it rose and have come to worship him."
Matthew 2:2

The wise men did not regard the favor of seeing the star as a matter to be rested in. They did not say, "We have seen his star, and that is enough." Many say, "Well, we attend a place of worship regularly, is not that enough?" There are those who say, "We were baptized, baptism brought regeneration with it; we come to the sacrament, and do we not get grace through it?" Poor souls! The star which leads to Christ they mistake for Christ himself, and worship the star instead of the Lord. O may none of you ever be so foolish as to rest in outward ordinances! God will say to you, if you depend upon sacraments or upon public worship, "Bring no more vain offerings; incense is an abomination to me" (Isaiah 1:13). "Who has required of you this trampling of my courts?" (v. 12).

What does God care for outward forms and ceremonies? When I see men putting on white gowns, and scarfs and bands, and singing their prayers, and bowing and scraping, I wonder what sort of god it is they worship. Surely, he must have more affinity with the gods of the heathen than with the great Jehovah who has made the heavens and the earth. Mark well the exceeding glory of Jehovah's works on sea and land. Behold the heavens and their countless hosts of stars, hark to the howling of the winds and the rush of the hurricane, think of him who makes the clouds his chariot, and rides on the wings of the wind, and then consider whether this infinite God is a being to whom it is a matter of grave consequence whether a cup of wine is lifted in worship as high as a man's hair or only as high as his nose! O foolish generation, to think that Jehovah is contained in your temples made with hands, and that he cares for your vestments, your processions, your postures, and your genuflections. You fight over your ritual, even to its jots and tittles do you consider it. Surely you know not the glorious Jehovah, if you conceive that these things yield any pleasure to him. No, beloved, we desire to worship the Most High in all simplicity and earnestness of spirit, and never to stop in the outward form, lest we be foolish enough to think that to see the star is sufficient, and therefore fail to find the incarnate God.

Note well, that these wise men did not find satisfaction in what they had themselves done to reach the child. As we have observed, they may have come hundreds of miles, but they did not mention it; they did not sit down and say, "Well, we have journeyed across deserts, over hills, and across rivers, it is enough." No, they must find the newborn King, nothing else would satisfy them. Do not say, dear hearer, "I have been praying now for months, I have been searching the Scriptures for weeks, to find the Savior." I am glad you have done so, but do not rest in it. You must get Christ, or else you perish after all your exertion and your trouble. Jesus you want, nothing more than Jesus, but nothing less than Jesus. Nor must you be satisfied with travelling in the way the star would lead you. You must reach HIM. Do not stop short of eternal life. Lay hold on it, not merely seek it and long for it, but lay hold on eternal life, and do not be content until it is an ascertained fact with you that Jesus Christ is yours.

I should like you to notice how these wise men were not satisfied with merely getting to Jerusalem. They might have said, "Ah! now we are in the land where the Child is born, we will be thankful and sit down." No, but "Where is he?" He is born at Bethlehem. Well, they get to Bethlehem, but we do not find that when they reached that village they said, "This is a favored spot, we will sit down here." Not at all, they wanted to know where the house was. They reached the house, and the star got over it. It was a fair sight to see the cottage with the star above it, and to think that the newborn King was there, but that did not satisfy them. No, they went right into the house. They did not rest till they saw the Child himself, and had worshipped him.

I pray that you and I may always be so led by the Spirit of God that we may never put up with anything short of a real grasping of Christ, a believing sight of Christ as a Savior, as our Savior, as our Savior even now. If there be one danger above another that the young seeker should strive against, it is the danger of stopping short of a hearty faith in Jesus Christ. While your heart is tender like wax, take care that no seal but the seal of

Christ be set on you. Now that you are uneasy and out of comfort, make this your vow, "I will not be comforted till Jesus comforts me." It would be better for you never to be awakened than to be lulled to sleep by Satan—for a sleep that follows upon a partial conviction is generally a deeper slumber than any other that falls upon the sons of men.

My soul, I charge you get to the blood of Christ, and be washed in it; get to the life of Christ, and let that life be in you, that you be indeed God's child. Put not up with suppositions, be not satisfied with appearances and maybes; rest nowhere till you have said—God having given you the faith to say it, "He loved me and gave himself for me" (Galatians 2:20), "[he] is all my salvation and all my desire" (2 Samuel 23:5 KJV). See, then, how these wise men were not made by the sight of the star to keep away from Christ, but they were encouraged by it to come to Christ, and do you be encouraged, dear seeker, this morning to come to Jesus by the fact that you are blessed with the gospel. You have an invitation given you to come to Jesus, you have the motions of God's Spirit upon your conscience, awakening you; O come, come and welcome, and let this strange winter's day be a day of brightness and of gladness to a many a seeking soul.

Day 15

The First Christmas Carol

"Glory to God in the highest, and on earth
peace among those with whom he is pleased!"
Luke 2:14

What is the instructive lesson to be learned from this first syllable of the angels' song? Why this, that salvation is God's highest glory. He is glorified in every dew drop that twinkles to the morning sun. He is magnified in every wood flower that blossoms in the copse, although it live to blush unseen, and waste its sweetness in the forest air. God is glorified in every bird that warbles on the spray; in every lamb that skips the mead. Do not the fishes in the sea praise him. From the tiny minnow to the huge Leviathan, do not all creatures that swim the water bless and praise his name? Do not all created things extol him? Is there anything beneath the sky, save man, that does not glorify God? Do not the stars exalt him, when they write his name upon the azure of heaven in their golden letters? Do not the lightnings adore him when they flash his brightness in arrows of light piercing the midnight darkness? Do not thunders extol him when they roll like drums in the march of the God of armies? Do not all things exalt him, from the least even to the greatest?

But sing, sing, oh universe, till you have exhausted yourself, you cannot afford a song so sweet as the song of incarnation. Though creation may be a majestic organ of praise, it cannot reach the compass of the golden canticle—incarnation! There is more in that than in creation, more melody in Jesus in the manger, than there is in worlds on worlds rolling their grandeur round the throne of the Most High.

Pause Christian and consider this a minute. See how every attribute is here magnified. Lo! what wisdom is here. God becomes man that God may be just, and the justifier of the ungodly. Lo! what power, for where is power so great as when it conceals power? What power, that Godhead should unrobe and become man! Behold, what love is thus revealed to us when Jesus becomes a man. Behold, what faithfulness! How many promises are this day kept? How many solemn obligations are this hour discharged? Tell me one attribute of God that is not manifest in Jesus, and your ignorance shall be the reason why you have not seen it so. The whole of God is glorified in Christ; and though some part of the name of God is written in the universe, it is here best read—in Him who was the Son of Man, and, yet, the Son of God.

Friends, does not this verse, this song of angels, stir your heart with happiness? When I read that, and found the angels singing it, I thought to myself, "Then if the angels ushered in the gospel's great Head with singing, ought I not to preach with singing? And ought not my readers to live with singing? Ought not their hearts to be glad and their spirits to rejoice?" Well, thought I, there be some somber religionists who were born in a dark night in December that think a smile upon the face is wicked, and believe that for a Christian to be glad and rejoice is to be inconsistent. Ah! I wish these gentlemen had seen the angels when they sang about Christ. For if angels sang about his birth, though it was no concern of theirs, certainly men ought to sing about it as long as they live, sing about it when they die, and sing about it when they live in heaven for ever. I do long to see in the midst of the church more of a singing Christianity.

The last few years have been breeding in our midst a groaning and unbelieving Christianity. Now, I doubt not its sincerity, but I do doubt its healthy character. I say it may be true and real enough; God forbid I should say a word against the sincerity of those who practice it; but it is a sickly religion. Watts hit the mark when he said,

> Religion never was designed
> To make our pleasures less.

It is designed to do away with some of our pleasures, but it gives us many more, to make up for what it takes away; so it does not make them less. O you that see in Christ nothing but a subject to stimulate your doubts and make the tears run down your cheeks; O ye that always say,

> Lord, what a wretched land is this,
> That yields us no supplies.

Come here and see the angels. Do they tell their story with groans, and sobs, and sighs? Ah, no; they shout aloud, "Glory to God in the highest." Now, imitate them, my dear brothers and sisters. If you are professors of religion, try always to have a cheerful carriage. Let others mourn; but

> Why should the children of a king
> Go mourning all their days?

Anoint your head and wash your face; appear not unto men to fast (Matthew 6:17). Rejoice in the Lord always, and again I will say, rejoice (Philippians 4:4). Specially this week be not ashamed to be glad. You need not think it a wicked thing to be happy. Penance and whipping and misery are no such very virtuous things, after all. The damned are miserable; let the saved be happy. Why should you hold fellowship with the lost by feelings of perpetual mourning? Why not rather anticipate the joys of heaven, and begin to sing on earth that song which you will never need to end?

Day 16
The Holy Servant Jesus

"While you stretch out your hand to heal,
and signs and wonders are performed through
the name of your holy servant Jesus."
Acts 4:30

Dear friends, may our hearts be enlightened to see, as the apostles did, the beauty and excellence of the real humanity of our Lord and Savior Jesus Christ. While we always contend that Christ is God, very God of very God, let us never lose the firm conviction he is most certainly and truly a man. He is not a God humanized, nor yet a human being deified; but, as to his Godhead, pure Godhead, equal and co-eternal with the Father; as to his manhood, perfect manhood; made in all respects like unto the rest of mankind, sin alone excepted.

His humanity was real, for he was born. He lay hidden in the virgin's womb, and in due time was born into a world of suffering. The gate by which we enter upon the first life, he passed through also; he was not created, nor transformed, but his humanity was begotten and born. As he was born, so in the circumstances of his birth, he is completely human. He is as weak and feeble as any other babe. He is not even royal, but human. Those who were born in marble halls of old were wrapped in purple garments, and were thought by the vulgar to be a superior race; but this babe is wrapped in swaddling clothes and has a manger for his cradle, that the true humanness of his being may come out.

More a man than he is a Prince of the House of David, he knows the woes of a peasant's child. As he grows up, the very growth shows how completely human he is. He does not spring into full manhood at once, but he grows in stature, and in favor both with God and man. When he reaches man's estate, he gets the common stamp of manhood upon his brow. "By the sweat of your face you shall eat bread" (Genesis 3:19) is the common heritage of us all, and he receives no better. The carpenter's shop must witness to the toils of a Savior, and when he becomes the preacher and the prophet, still we read such significant words as these—"Jesus, wearied as he was from his journey, was sitting beside the well" (John 4:6). We find him needing to betake himself to rest in sleep, he slumbers at the stern of the vessel when it is tossed in the midst of the tempest (Mark 4:38).

Brothers and sisters, if sorrow be the mark of real manhood, and "man is born to trouble as the sparks fly upward" (Job 5:7), certainly Jesus Christ has the truest evidence of being a man. If to hunger and to thirst be signs that he was no shadow, and his manhood no fiction, you have these. If to associate with his fellow men, and eat and drink as they did, will be proof to your mind that he was none other than a man, you see him sitting at a feast one day, at another time he graces a marriage supper, and on another occasion he is hungry, and "has nowhere to lay his head" (Luke 9:58).

Since the day when the prince of the power of the air obtained dominion in this world, men are tempted, and he, though he is born pure and holy, must not be delivered from temptation.

> The desert his temptation knew
> His conflict and his victory too.

The garden marked the bloody sweat, as it started from every pore while he endured the agony of conflict with the prince of this world. If, since we have fallen and must endure temptation, we have need to pray, so had he—

> Cold mountains and the midnight air
> Witnessed the fervor of his prayer.

Strong crying and tears go up to heaven mingled with his pleas and entreaties, and what clearer proof could we have of his being man of the substance of his mother, and man like ourselves, than this, that he was heard in that he feared. There appeared unto him an angel strengthening him; to whom but men are angels ministering spirits? Brothers and sisters, we have never discovered the weakness of our manhood more than when God has deserted us. When the spiritual consolations which comforted us have been withdrawn, and the light of God's face has been hidden from us, then we have said, "I am a worm and not a man" (Psalm 22:6), and out of the dust and ashes of human weakness have we cried unto the Most High God. Let "Eloi! Eloi! lema sabachthani" (Mark 15:34) assure you that Christ has felt the same.

Follow man wherever you will, and you find the footprint of the Son of Mary. Go after man where you will, into scenes of sorrow of every hue, and you shall find traces of Jesus's pilgrimage there. You shall find in whatever struggle and conflict of which man is capable, the Captain of our salvation has had a share. Leave out sin, and Christ is the perfect picture of humanity. Simple as the truth is, and lying as it does at the very basis of our Christianity, yet let us not despise it, but try to get a personal grip of it if we can.

Jesus, my mediator, is a man, "Immanuel, God with us." He is a child born, he is better than that, for "to us a child is born, to us a son is given" (Isaiah 9:6). He is to us a brother; he is bone of our bone today. As a man leaves his father and mother and cleaves to his wife, and the two become one flesh, so has he left the glory of his Father's house and become one flesh with his people (Ephesians 5:31–32). Flesh, and bone, and blood, and heart, that may ache and suffer, and be broken and be bruised, yea, and may die, such is Jesus; for here he completes the picture. As the whole human race must yield its neck to the great iron-crowned monarch of death, so must Christ himself say, "Father, into your hands I commit my spirit" (Luke 23:46), and he, too, must yield up the ghost. Oh, Christian, see your nearness to him and be glad this morning! Oh, sinner, see his nearness to you! Come to him with confidence, for in body and soul he is completely human.

Day 17

Humanity's Glory Restored

> But we see him who for a little while was made
> lower than the angels, namely Jesus, crowned with glory
> and honor because of the suffering of death, so that
> by the grace of God he might taste death for everyone.
> Hebrews 2:9

See the glory of manhood now restored! Man was but a little lower than the angels, and had dominion over the fowl of the air, and over the fish of the sea. That royalty he lost; the crown was taken from his head by the hand of sin, and the beauty of the image of God was dashed by his rebellion. But all this is given back to us. We see Jesus, who was made a little lower than the angels, for the suffering of death, crowned with glory and honor (Hebrews 2:9); and at this day all things are put under him, waiting, as he does, and expecting the time when all his enemies shall be beneath his feet, and the last enemy, Death, shall be destroyed by man (1 Corinthians 15:25–26)—by the very man whom he boasted that he had destroyed.

It is our nature, brothers and sisters, Jesus in our manhood, who is now Lord of providence; it is our nature which has hanging at its girdle the sovereign keys of heaven, and earth, and hell; it is our nature which sits upon the throne of God at this very day. No angel ever sat upon God's throne, but a man has done it, and is doing it now. Of no angel was it ever said, "You will be King of kings and Lord of lords; 'May desert tribes

bow down before him, and his enemies lick the dust!'"
(Psalm 72:9). But this is said of a man. It is a man who
shall judge the world in righteousness; a man who shall
distribute crowns of reward; a man who shall denounce,
"Depart from me, you cursed" (Matthew 25:41); a man,
the thunder of whose words shall make hell shrink with
affright. Oh, how glorious is renovated manhood! What
an honor is it to be man, not of the fallen first Adam,
but man made in the image in the second Adam? Let us
with all our weakness, and infirmity, and imperfection,
yet bless and praise God, who made us what we are by
his grace, for man, in the person of Christ, is second
only to God—nay, is in such union with God, that he
cannot be nearer to him.

When we think of the true and proper manhood of
Christ, ought we not to rejoice that a blessed channel is
opened by which God's mercy can come to us? "How
can God reach man?" was once the question. But now,
there is another question, "How can God refuse to bless
those men who are in Christ?" The everlasting Father
must bless his only-begotten Son, and in blessing him
he has blessed a man, and that man having all the elect
in him, they are necessarily all blessed in him. Look
upon the person of Christ as that of a representative
individual. Whatever Christ is, all his elect are, just as
whatever Adam was all men who were in him became.
If Adam fell, all manhood fell; if Christ stands and is
honored and glorified, then all who are in Christ, that is
the goodly fellowship of his elect, are all blessed in him.

Now, it is utterly impossible, but that God should
bless Jesus Christ, for Jesus Christ is forever one with

God, and his manhood is also one with God-head. As an old writer observes, "The nearest union that we know of is the union between the humanity and the divinity in the person of Christ. That of the three persons in the Trinity may rather be called a unity than a union—but this is the closest union we know of—the union between humanity and deity in Christ." So complete is it, that you cannot think of Christ aright as a man apart from God, nor as God apart from man. The very idea of Christ has in it the two natures, and it is a clear impossibility that the Godhead should not impart of its blessedness to the manhood, and that manhood being thus blessed, every elect soul is necessarily blessed also. O see what a channel is thus opened; a channel through which the stream cannot but flow; a golden pipe through which grace cannot but come. The laws of nature might be reversed, but not the laws of God's nature, and it is a law of God's nature that in the person of Christ the deity must bless the manhood, and that manhood being blessed, it is another law that elect manhood must be blessed, since that elect manhood is forever indissolubly bound up with the person of the Lord Jesus Christ. See what a river deep and broad is here opened for us, and what a fullness there is in that river, for all the fullness of the deity dwells in Christ, and the fullness of that deity thus flows to man.

See again, beloved, what a door of access is thus opened between us and God! I am a man; Christ is a man. I come to the man Christ Jesus—no I have not even to do that—I am in the man Christ. If I am a believer, I am a portion of him. Well, being a portion of the man Christ, and God being united with him,

I am very near unto God. I have such nearness of access then to God, that whatever may be my desires and my prayers, I have no need to climb to heaven nor to descend into the depth in order to obtain my desire, for God's ear must be near to me inasmuch as God is in Christ, and my soul being in Christ I am very, very near to God. Christ's body is the veil that hangs before the majesty of God, that veil was rent; and whoever by a living faith knows how to come through the rent body of the man, Christ, comes at once into the presence of God. Such communion, such sacred commerce, such blessed interchanges between mankind and God could never have taken place on any other plan.

Another thing I cannot leave out, is this—beloved, do see it, do see it—how safe we are! Our soul's estate was once put in the hands of Adam. He was a fallible man; how unsafe our salvation was then! The salvation of every believer now is in the hand of a man; it is the man Christ Jesus! But what a man! Can he fail? Can he sin? Can he fall? O no, beloved, for the deity is in intimate union with the manhood, and the man Christ Jesus, since he can never sin, can never fall, and is therefore a sure foundation for the perpetual salvation of all the elect. Beloved, our salvation does not rest with ourselves, we may have all the joy of perfect security, because it rests in the hand of one who cannot by any possibility sin, who cannot err, cannot fail, but who stands fast forever, from everlasting to everlasting.

Day 18
Holy Work for Christmas

And the shepherds returned, glorifying and praising God
for all they had heard and seen, as it had been told them.
Luke 2:20

"The shepherds returned," we read in the twentieth verse, "glorifying and praising God for all they had heard and seen, as it had been told them." Returned to what? Returned to business to look after the lambs and sheep again. Then if we desire to glorify God we need not give up our business. Some people get the notion into their heads that the only way in which they can live for God is by becoming ministers, missionaries, or Bible women. Alas! how many of us would be shut out from any opportunity of magnifying the Most High if this were the case. The shepherds went back to the sheep-pens glorifying and praising God.

Beloved, it is not office, it is earnestness; it is not position, it is grace which will enable us to glorify God. God is most surely glorified in that cobbler's stall where the godly worker as he plies the awl sings of the Savior's love, ay, glorified far more than in many a priestly office where official religiousness performs its scanty duties. The name of Jesus is glorified by yonder carter as he drives his horse and blesses his God, or speaks to his fellow laborer by the roadside, as much as by yonder theologian who, throughout the country like Boanerges, is thundering out the gospel. God is glorified by our abiding in our vocation. Take care you do not fall out of the path of duty by leaving your calling, and take care you do not dishonor your profession while in it. Think not much of yourselves, but do not think too little of your callings.

There is no trade which is not sanctified by the gospel. If you turn to the Bible, you will find the most menial forms of labor have been in some way or other connected either with the most daring deeds of faith, or else with persons whose lives have been otherwise illustrious. Keep to your calling, brothers and sisters, keep to your calling! Whatever God has made you, when he calls you, abide in that, focus on that, unless you are quite sure that he calls you to something else. The shepherds glorified God though they went to their trade.

They glorified God though they were shepherds. As we remarked, they were not men of learning. So far from having an extensive library full of books, it is probable they could not read a word; yet they glorified God. This takes away all excuse for you good people who say, "I am no scholar; I never had any education; I never went even to a Sunday-school." Ah, but if your heart is right, you can glorify God. Never mind, Sarah, do not be cast down because you know so little; learn more if you can, but make good use of what you do know. Never mind, John; it is indeed a pity that you should have had to toil so early, as not to have acquired even the rudiments of knowledge; but do not think that you cannot glorify God. If you would praise God, live a holy life; you can do that by his grace, at any rate, without scholarship. If you would do good to others, be good yourself; and that is a way which is as open to the most illiterate as it is to the best taught. Be of good courage!

Shepherds glorified God, and so may you. Remember there is one thing in which they had a preference over the wise men. The wise men wanted a star to lead them; the shepherds did not. The wise men went wrong even with a star, stumbled into Jerusalem; the shepherds went straight away to Bethlehem. Simple minds sometimes find a glorified Christ where learned heads, much puzzled with their lore, miss him. A good doctor used to say, "Lo, these simpletons have entered into the kingdom, while we learned men have been fumbling for the latch." It is often so; and so, you, simple minds, be comforted and glad.

The way in which these shepherds honored God is worth noticing. They did it by praising him. Let us think more of sacred song than we sometimes do. When the song is bursting in full chorus from the thousands in this house, it is but a noise in the ear of some men; but inasmuch as many true hearts, touched with the love of Jesus, are keeping pace with their tongues, it is not a mere noise in God's esteem, there is a sweet music in it that makes glad his ear.

What is the great goal of all Christian effort? When I stood here the other morning preaching the gospel, my mind was fully exercised with the winning of souls, but I seemed while preaching to get beyond that. I thought, *Well, that is not the chief end after all—the chief end is to glorify God, and even the saving of sinners is sought by the rightminded as the means to that end.* Then it struck me all of a sudden, *If in psalm singing and hymn singing we do really glorify God, we are doing more than in the preaching; because we are not then in the means, we are close upon the great end itself.* If we praise God with heart and tongue we glorify him in the surest possible manner, we are really glorifying him then.

"The one who offers thanksgiving as his sacrifice glorifies me," says the Lord (Psalm 50:23). Sing then, my brothers and sisters! Sing not only when you are together but sing alone. Cheer your labor with psalms, and hymns, and spiritual songs. Make glad the family with sacred music. We sing too little, I am sure, yet the revival of religion has always been attended with the revival of Christian psalmody. Luther's translations of the psalms were of as much service as Luther's discussions and controversies; and the hymns of Charles Wesley, and Cennick and Toplady, and Newton, and Cowper, aided as much in the quickening of spiritual life in England as the preaching of John Wesley and George Whitefield. We want more singing. Sing more and murmur less, sing more and slander less, sing more and cavil [complain] less, sing more and mourn less. God grant us today, as these shepherds did, to glorify God by praising him.

Day 19

The First Recorded Words of Jesus

*And when his parents saw him, they were astonished.
And his mother said to him, "Son, why have you treated us so?
Behold, your father and I have been searching for you in great
distress." And he said to them, "Why were you looking for me?
Did you not know that I must be in my Father's house?"*
Luke 2:48–49

Notice, first, that he evidently perceived most clearly his high relationship. Mary said, "Your father and I have been searching for you in great distress." The child Jesus had been accustomed to call Joseph his father, no doubt, and Joseph was his father in the common belief of those round about him. We read in reference to our Lord, even at thirty years of age, these words: "being the son (as was supposed) of Joseph" (Luke 3:23). The holy child does not deny it, but he looks over the head of Joseph, and he brings before his mother's mind another Father. "Did you not know that I must be about My Father's business?" (Luke 2:49 NKJV)

He does not explain this saying, but it is evident enough that he remembered then the wonderful relationship which existed between his humanity and the great God; for he was not conceived after the ordinary manner, but he had come into the world in such a fashion that it was said to Mary, "The child to be born will be called holy—the Son of God" (Luke 1:35). In a still higher sense and as a divine being, he claimed Sonship with the Most High. But here no doubt he speaks as a man, and as a man he calls God "My Father," after a higher fashion than we can do, because of his mysterious birth. You notice that all through his life he never calls God "Our Father," although he bids us do so. We are children of the same family, and when we pray, we are to say, "Our Father in heaven" (Matthew 6:9). But our Lord Jesus has still a Sonship more special than ours, and therefore to God he says on his own account, "My Father." He expressly claims this personal relationship for himself, and I am sure we do not grudge him that relationship, for upon it our own relationship to the Father depends. Because he is the Son of the Highest, therefore we enter into the filial relationship with the Eternal One, according to our capacity. Jesus the child perceived that he was the Son of the Highest, and with all the simplicity of childhood he declared the secret to his mother, who already knew how true it was.

Brothers and sisters, this holy child's perception should be an instruction to us. Do you and I often enough and clearly enough perceive that God is our Father too? Do we not often act upon the hypothesis that we are not related to him, or that we are orphans, and that our Father in heaven is dead? Do you not catch yourselves sometimes departing from under the influence of the spirit of adoption and getting into the spirit of independence, and so of waywardness and sin? This will never do. Let us learn from this blessed One that as he early perceived his high and eminent relationship to the Father. So ought we to do, even though we may be nothing more than children in grace. We ought to know and to value beyond all expression our sonship with the great Father who is in heaven. This truth should override every other, and we should live and move and act under the consciousness of our being the children of God. O Holy Spirit, teach us this!

The child Jesus began also to perceive that he himself personally had a work to do, and so he said, "Did you not know that I must be about my Father's business?" He had been twelve years silent, but now the shadow of the cross began to fall upon him! And he felt a little of the burden of his life-work. He perceives that he has not come here merely to work in a carpenter's shop, or to be a peasant child at Nazareth. He has come here to vindicate the honor of God, to redeem his people, to save them from their sins, and to lead an army of blood-washed ones up to the throne of the great Father above, and, therefore, he declares that he has a higher occupation than Mary and Joseph can understand.

Yet he must go back to the home at Nazareth, and for eighteen years he must do his Father's business by, as far as we read, doing nothing in the way of public ministry. He must do his Father's business by hearing the Father, in secret, so that when he comes out he may say to his disciples, "All that I have heard from my Father I have made known to you" (John 15:15). So great a lesson had he to teach that he must spend another eighteen years in learning it fully, and God must open his ear, and waken him morning by morning to hear as an instructed one, that afterwards he may come forth the teacher of Israel, the Lord and Master of apostles and evangelists.

Beloved, I come back to the practical point again. Have you with your sonship obtained a vivid perception of your call and your work? You have not redemption set before you to accomplish, but you have to make known that redemption far and wide. As God has given to Christ authority over all flesh that he may give eternal life to as many as the Father has given him (John 17:2), so has Jesus given you power over such and such flesh, and there are some in this world who never will receive eternal life except through you. It is appointed that from your lips they shall hear the gospel; it is ordained in the divine decree that through your instrumentality they shall be brought into the kingdom of God. It is time that you and I, who perhaps have reached thirty, forty, fifty, or sixty years, should now bestir ourselves and say, "Did you not know that I must be up and doing in my Father's business?" David had to wait till he heard the sound of a going in the tops of the mulberry trees (2 Samuel 5:23–24); do you not hear the sound of a going now? Are there not signs and indications that you must work the will of him that sent you, and must finish his work? The night is coming when no one can work (John 9:4). Up, then, you children of God, and following the holy child Jesus, begin to put this question: "Did you not know that I must be about my Father's business?"

Day 20

The Empty Place

The king sat on his seat, as at other times,
on the seat by the wall. Jonathan sat opposite,
and Abner sat by Saul's side, but David's place was empty.
1 Samuel 20:25

Beloved, some day, when you will be keeping the Christmas feast, there will be many family gatherings, and in those family gatherings there will be some households where a place will be empty.

As I came here, I was thinking of what inroads death has made in this congregation this year. There have been many vacancies made, and there will be many more next year. I miss from one seat, a sister whom I saw upon her dying bed; and, from another part of the building, a brother whose cheering words in his last moments did my soul good. I miss here one and there another. I could run my finger along these pews in the area, and I could come up on this platform, and I could truly say, concerning one who has been called home this year, "David's place is empty." We can hardly say that literally, because his son fills it, and long may he fill it, and have God's blessing resting upon him! But here and there, and everywhere in this Tabernacle, I miss some who have gone home. Our family gathering is gradually breaking up; thank God, it is being reformed up yonder, where there will be no death and no parting.

When you get to your family gathering, perhaps you will have to remember that your mother has died this year, or it may be that your father has gone home, or perhaps it was the eldest son, or that sweet curly-headed child. Perhaps, tomorrow, you will be merry; and I do not say to you, "Be not so," but let these memories come over you, let them direct your thoughts upward, let them remind you that family gatherings are only for a time, and that the great gathering is above. There the immortals meet, there the feast never ends. Look away from earth with all its joys. Let them that have wives be as those that have none, let them that have children look on their children as dying ones (1 Corinthians 7:29–31). Let kinships, and friendships, and all these things, be regarded as they are, as vapor, as things that perish in the using. Hear the trumpet sound, "Up and away," and let your hearts be where Jesus is, and let your treasure be there also. Those dear ones who are in heaven beckon us to follow them, and we signal to tell them that we are on the way. Surely, they must look upon us with amazement if they see us hugging the things of earth as though we were to stay here forever. Let our conversation be in heaven, and let our affection be set on things above, and not on things on the earth.

My last reflection is this: there will be no empty place in heaven. In that great family gathering up above, they will not be able to say, "David's place is empty."

Beloved, if you are a believer in Christ, if you are the poorest saint, and the least worthy of consideration in the whole household, yet you shall have your place in heaven. You must have it, for God will not have one empty seat there, and nobody but yourself can fill your place. Our Lord Jesus Christ says—mark his words—"I go to prepare a place." That is something; but note the next words, "I go to prepare a place for you" for you, not for somebody else, but for you (John 14:2). If you are a believer in Jesus Christ, you must have the place which Jesus Christ has gone to prepare for you. There is a crown in heaven which can fit no other head but mine; and there is a harp in heaven out of which no other fingers but mine can bring music. There is a mansion in the skies which nobody but you can ever occupy; and there are joys for you only, and a place in the complete circle of God's elect that must be filled, and must be filled by you. Oh, what joy is this! Press onward, my brother, go on bravely; if the darkness thickens, and the dangers multiply, Christ is your life, and you cannot die. The everlasting wings shall cover you, and the everlasting arms shall be underneath you. You shall meet us in the place where all the family shall be present, and the great Father and the elder Brother shall welcome them all, and no "David's place" shall be empty. May I be there, may we all be there; and God shall have the praise! Amen and amen.

Day 21
The Exaltation of Christ

Therefore God has highly exalted him and bestowed on him
the name that is above every name, so that at the name
of Jesus every knee should bow, in heaven and on earth
and under the earth, and every tongue confess that
Jesus Christ is Lord, to the glory of God the Father.
Philippians 2:9–11

Here also is the very fountain and well-spring of joy, in the reason of Christ's exaltation. "Therefore God has highly exalted him." Why? Because, "though he was in the form of God, did not count equality with God a thing to be grasped, but emptied himself, by taking the form of a servant, being born in the likeness of men. And being found in human form, he humbled himself by becoming obedient to the point of death, even death on a cross" (Philippians 2:6–8). This of course relates to the manhood of our Lord Jesus Christ.

As God, Christ needed no exaltation; he was higher than the highest, "God over all, blessed forever" (Romans 9:5). But the symbols of his glory having been for a while obscured, having wrapped his Godhead in mortal flesh, his flesh with his Godhead ascended up on high, and the man-God, Christ Jesus, who had stooped to shame, and sorrow, and degradation, was highly exalted, "far above all rule and authority" (Ephesians 1:21) that he might reign Prince-Regent over all worlds, yea, over heaven itself.

Let us consider, for a moment, that depth of degradation to which Christ descended; and then, my beloved, it will give you joy to think, that for that very reason his manhood was highly exalted. Do you see that man—

The humble Man before his foes,
The weary Man and full of woes?

Do you mark him as he speaks? Note the marvelous eloquence which pours from his lips, and see how the crowds attend him? But do you hear, in the distance, the growling of the thunders of calumny and scorn? Listen to the words of his accusers. They say he is "a glutton and a drunkard, a friend of tax collectors and sinners" (Matthew 11:19); "he has a demon, and is insane" (John 10:20). All the whole vocabulary of abuse is exhausted by insults upon him. He is slandered, abused, persecuted! Stop! Do you think that he is by this cast down, by this degraded? No, for this very reason: "God has highly exalted him." Mark the shame and spitting that have come upon the cheek of the Man of Sorrows! See his hair plucked with cruel hands; mark how they torture him and how they mock him. Do you think that this is all dishonorable to Christ? It is apparently so; but listen to this: "He humbled himself by becoming obedient," and therefore "God has highly exalted him." Ah! there is a marvelous connection between that shame and spitting, and the bending of the knee of seraphs. There is a strange yet mystic link which unites the calumny and the slander with the choral sympathies of adoring angels. The one was, as it were, the seed of the other. Strange that it should be, but the black, the bitter seed brought forth a sweet and glorious flower which blooms forever. He suffered and he reigned; he stooped to conquer, and he conquered for he stooped, and was exalted for he conquered.

Consider him further still. Do you mark him in your imagination nailed to yonder cross! O eyes! you are full of pity, with tears standing thick! Oh! How I mark the floods gushing down his cheeks! Do you see his hands bleeding, and his feet too, gushing gore? Behold him! The bulls of Bashan gird him round (Psalm 22:12), and the dogs are hounding him to death! Hear him! "Eloi, Eloi, lama sabachthani?" (Mark 15:34). The earth startles with affright. A God is groaning on a cross! What! Does not this dishonor Christ? No; it honors him! Each of the thorns becomes a brilliant gem in his diadem of glory; the nails are forged into his scepter, and his wounds do clothe him with the purple of empire. The treading of the winepress has stained his garments (Isaiah 63:3), but not with stains of scorn and dishonor. The stains are embroideries upon his royal robes forever. The treading of that winepress has made his garments purple with the empire of a world; and he is the Master of a universe forever.

O Christian! sit down and consider that your Master did not mount from earth's mountains into heaven, but from her valleys. It was not from heights of bliss on earth that he strode to bliss eternal, but from depths of woe he mounted up to glory. Oh! what a stride was that, when, at one mighty step from the grave to the throne of The Highest, the man Christ, the God, did gloriously ascend. And yet reflect! He in some way, mysterious yet true, was exalted because he suffered. "Being found in human form, he humbled himself by becoming obedient to the point of death, even death on a cross. Therefore God has highly exalted him and bestowed on him the name that is above every name."

Believer, there is comfort for you here, if you will take it. If Christ was exalted through his degradation, so shall you be. Count not your steps to triumph by your steps upward, but by those which are seemingly downward. The way to heaven is downhill. He who would be honored forever must sink in his own esteem, and often in that of his fellow men. Oh! think not of the fool who is mounting to heaven by his own light opinions of himself and by the flatteries of his fellows, that he shall safely reach Paradise. No, that on which he rests shall burst, and he shall fall and be broken in pieces. But he who descends into the mines of suffering, shall find unbounded riches there; and he who dives into the depths of grief, shall find the pearl of everlasting life within its caverns.

Day 22

The Mystery of Godliness

Great indeed, we confess, is the mystery of godliness:
He was manifested in the flesh.
1 Timothy 3:16

"God was manifest in the flesh" (1 Timothy 3:16 KJV). I believe that our version is the correct one, but the fiercest battles have been held over this sentence. It is asserted that the word *Theos* is a corruption for *Os*, so that, instead of reading "God was manifest in the flesh," we should read, "who was manifest in the flesh."

There is very little occasion for fighting about this matter, for if the text does not say "God was manifest in the flesh," who does it say was manifest in the flesh? Either a man, or an angel, or a devil. Does it tell us that a man was manifest in the flesh? Assuredly that cannot be its teaching, for every man is manifest in the flesh, and there is no sense whatever in making such a statement concerning any mere man, and then calling it a mystery. Was it an angel, then? But what angel was ever manifest in the flesh? And if he were, would it be at all a mystery that he should be "seen by angels" (1 Timothy 3:16)? Is it a wonder for an angel to see an angel? Can it be that the devil was manifest in the flesh? If so, he has been "taken up in glory" (1 Timothy 3:16) which, let us hope, is not the case.

Well, if it was neither a man, nor an angel, nor a devil, who was manifest in the flesh, then surely, he must have been God; and so, if the word be not there, the sense must be there, or else nonsense. We believe that, if criticism should grind the text in a mill, it would get out of it no more and no less than the sense expressed by our grand old version. God himself was manifest in the flesh. What a mystery is this! A mystery of mysteries! God the invisible was manifest; God the spiritual dwelt in flesh; God the infinite, uncontained, boundless, was manifest in the flesh. What infinite leagues our thought must traverse between Godhead self-existent, and, therefore, full of power and self-sufficiency, before we have descended to the far-down level of poor flesh, which is as grass at its best, and dust in its essence! Where find we a greater contrast than between God and flesh, and yet the two are blended in the incarnation of the Savior. God was manifest in the flesh; truly God, not God humanized, but God as God. He was manifest in real flesh; not in manhood deified and made superhuman, but in actual flesh.

> Oh joy! there sitteth in our flesh,
> Upon a throne of light,
> One of a human mother born,
> In perfect Godhead bright!
> For ever God, for ever man,
> My Jesus shall endure;
> And fix'd on Him, my hope remains
> Eternally secure.

Matchless truth, let the church never fail to set it forth, for it is essential to the world's salvation that this doctrine of the incarnation be made fully known.

O my brethren, since it is "great indeed," let us sit down and feed upon it. What a miracle of condescension is here, that God should manifest himself in flesh. It needs not so much to be preached upon as to be pondered in the heart. It needs that you sit down in quiet, and consider how he who made you became like you, he who is your God became your brother man. He who is adored of angels once lay in a manger; he who feeds all living things hungered and was athirst; he who oversees all worlds as God, was, as a man, made to sleep, to suffer, and to die like yourselves. This is a statement not easily to be believed. If he had not been beheld by many witnesses, so that men handled him, looked upon him, and heard him speak, it would be a thing not readily to be accepted, that so divine a person should be manifest in flesh. It is a wonder of condescension!

And it is a marvel, too, of benediction, for God's manifestation in human flesh conveys a thousand blessings to us. Bethlehem's star is the morning star of hope to believers. Now man is nearest to God. Never was God manifest in angel nature, but he is manifest in flesh. Now, between poor puny man that is born of a woman, and the infinite God, there is a bond of union of the most wonderful kind. God and man in one person is the Lord Jesus Christ! This brings our manhood near to God, and by so doing it ennobles our nature, it lifts us up from the dunghill and sets us among princes; while at the same time it enriches us by endowing our manhood with all the glory of Christ Jesus in whom dwelleth all the fullness of the Godhead bodily. Lift up your eyes, you down-trodden sons of man! If you be men, you have a brotherhood with Christ, and Christ is God. O you who have begun to despise yourselves and think that you are merely sent to be drudges upon earth, and slaves of sin! Lift up your heads and look for redemption in the Son of Man, who has broken the captives' bonds. If you be believers in the Christ of God, then are you also the children of God, and if children then heirs—heirs of God—joint heirs with Jesus Christ.

What a fullness of consolation there is in this truth, as well as of benediction; for if the Son of God be man, then he understands me and will have a fellow feeling for me. He knows my unfitness to worship sometimes—he knows my tendencies to grow weary and dull my pains, my trials, and my griefs:

> He knows what fierce temptations mean,
> For he has felt the same.

Man, truly man, yet sitting at the right hand of the Father, you, O Savior, are the delight of my soul. Is there not the richest comfort in this for you, the people of God?

Day 23

The Great Birthday
of Our Coming Age

But when the fullness of time had come,
God sent forth his Son, born of woman, born under the law,
to redeem those who were under the law,
so that we might receive adoption as sons.

Galatians 4:4–5

God sent his Son in real humanity—"born of woman." Perhaps you may get nearer to it if you say, "made to be born of woman," for both ideas are present, the being made and the being born. Christ was really and truly of the substance of his mother, as certainly as any other infant that is born into the world is so. God did not create the human nature of Christ apart, and then transmit it into mortal existence by some special means; but his Son was made and born of a woman. He is, therefore, of our race, a man like ourselves, and not man of another stock. You are to make no mistake about it: He is not only of humanity, but of your humanity; for that which is born of a woman is brother to us, be it born when it may.

Yet there is an omission, I doubt not intentional, to show how holy was that human nature, for he is born of a woman, not of a man. The Holy Spirit overshadowed the Virgin, and "that holy thing" (Luke 1:35 KJV) was born of her without the original sin which pertains to our race by natural descent. Here is a pure humanity though a true humanity; a true humanity though free from sin. Born of a woman, he was of few days and full of trouble (Job 14:1); born of a woman, he was compassed with our physical infirmities; but as he was not born of man he was altogether without tendency to evil or delight therein. I beg you to rejoice in this near approach of Christ to us. Ring out the glad bells, if not in the spires and steeples, yet within your own hearts; for gladder news did never greet your ear than this, that he that is the Son of God was also "born of woman."

Still further it is added, that God sent his Son made under the law or "born under the law"; for the word is the same in both cases; and by the same means by which he came to be of a woman he came under the law. And now admire and wonder! The Son of God has come under the law. He was the Law-Maker and the Law-Giver, and he is both the Judge of the law and the Executioner of the law, and yet he himself came under the law. No sooner was he born of a woman than he came under the law, and this voluntarily and yet necessarily. He willed to be a man, and being a man, he accepted the position, and stood in the place of man as subject to the law of the race. When they took him and circumcised him according to the law, it was publicly declared that he was under the law. During the rest of his life, you will observe how reverently he observed the commands of God. Even to the ceremonial law as it was given by Moses, he had scrupulous regard. He despised the traditions and superstitions of men, but for the rule of the dispensation he had a high respect.

By way of rendering service unto God on our behalf, he came under the moral law. He kept his

Father's commandments. He obeyed to the full both the first and the second tables [the Ten Commandments] (Exodus 20:3–17); for he loved God with all his heart, and his neighbor as himself (Mark 12:30–31). "I delight to do your will, O my God," says he, "your law is within my heart" (Psalm 40:8). He could truly say of the Father, "I always do the things that are pleasing to him" (John 8:29).

Yet it was a marvelous thing that the King of kings should be under the law; and especially that he should come under the penalty of the law as well as the service of it. "Being found in human form, he humbled himself by becoming obedient to the point of death, even death on a cross" (Philippians 2:8). As our Surety and Substitute he came under the curse of the law; being made a curse for us (Galatians 3:13). Having taken our place and espoused our nature, though without sin himself, he came under the rigorous demands of justice, and in due time he bowed his head to the sentence of death. "He laid down his life for us" (1 John 3:16). He died the just for the unjust, to bring us to God.

In this mystery of his incarnation, in this wonderful substitution of himself in the place of sinful men, lies the ground of that wonderful advance which believers made when Jesus came in the flesh. His advent in human form commenced the era of spiritual maturity and freedom. What else has he come for? Notice further, "that we might receive the adoption as sons." The Lord Jesus Christ has come in human flesh that his people might to the full realize, grasp, and enjoy, "the adoption as sons." I want you this morning to see if you can do that. May the Holy Spirit enable you. What is it to receive the adoption as sons? Why to feel, "Now I am under the mastery of love, as a dear child, who is both loved and loving. I go in and out of my Father's house not as a casual servant, called in by the day or the week, but as a child at home. I am not looking for hire as a servant, for I am ever with my Father, and all that he has is mine. My God is my Father, and his presence makes me glad (Psalm 21:6). I am not afraid of him, but I delight in him, for nothing can separate me from him (Romans 8:38–39). I feel a perfect love that casts out fear (1 John 4:18), and I delight myself in him."

Try now and enter into that spirit this morning. That is why Christ has come in the flesh—on purpose that you, his people, may be to the full the adopted children of the Lord, acting out and enjoying all the privileges which sonship secures to you.

Day 24
The Two Advents of Christ

And just as it is appointed for man to die once, and after that
comes judgment, so Christ, having been offered once to bear
the sins of many, will appear a second time, not to deal
with sin but to save those who are eagerly waiting for him.
Hebrews 9:27–28

In the prophecy of his coming the first and the second time there was disparity as well as correspondence. It's true in both cases he will come attended by angels, and the song shall be, "Glory to God in the highest, and on earth peace among those with whom he is pleased!" (Luke 2:14). It is true in both cases, shepherds who keep watch over their flocks even by night shall be among the first to hail him with their sleepless eyes—blessed shepherds who watch Christ's folds and therefore shall see the Great Shepherd when he comes (1 Peter 5:4).

Still, how different I say will be his coming. At first he came an infant of a span long; now he shall come "In rainbow-wreath and clouds of storm," the glorious one. Then he entered into a manger, now he shall ascend his throne. Then he sat upon a woman's knees, and did hang upon a woman's breast, now earth shall be at his feet and the whole universe shall hang upon his everlasting shoulders. Then he appeared the infant, now the infinite. Then he was born to trouble as the sparks fly upward, now he comes to glory as the lightning from one end of heaven to the other. A stable received him then; now the high arches of earth and heaven shall be too little for him. Horned oxen were then his companions, but now the chariots of God which are twenty thousand, even thousands of angels, shall be at his right hand. Then in poverty, his parents were too glad to receive the offerings of gold and frankincense and myrrh; but now in splendor, King of kings, and Lord of lords; all nations shall bow before him, and kings and princes shall pay homage at his feet. Still, he shall need nothing at their hands, for he will be able to say, "If I were hungry, I would not tell you, for the world and its fullness are mine" (Psalm 50:12). "You have put all things under his feet, all sheep and oxen, and also the beasts of the field" (Psalm 8:6–7).

Nor will there merely be a difference in his coming; there will be a most distinct and apparent difference in his person. He will be the same, so that we shall be able to recognize him as the Man of Nazareth, but O how changed! Where now the carpenter's smock? Royalty has now assumed its purple. Where now the toil-worn feet that needed to be washed after their long journeys of mercy? They are sandaled with light, they are "like burnished bronze, refined in a furnace" (Revelation 1:15). Where now the cry, "Foxes have holes and the birds of the air have nests, but the Son of Man has nowhere to lay his head" (Matthew 8:20)? Heaven is his throne; earth is his footstool (Isaiah 66:1). Methinks in the night visions, I behold the day dawning. And to the Son of Man there is given "dominion and glory and a kingdom, that all peoples, nations, and languages should serve him" (Daniel 7:14). Ah! who would think to recognize in the weary man and full of woes, the King eternal, immortal, invisible? Who would think that the humble man, despised and rejected, was the seed-corn out of which there should grow that full corn in the ear, Christ all-glorious, before whom the angels veil their faces and cry, "Holy, holy, holy, is the LORD of hosts!" (Isaiah 6:3)? He is the same, but yet how changed!

You that despised him, will you despise him now? Imagine the judgment day has come, and let this vast audience represent the gathering of the last dreadful morning. Now you who despised his cross, come forward and insult his throne! Now you who said he was a mere man, come near and resist him, while he proves himself to be your Creator! Now, you who said, "We will not have this man to reign over us" (Luke 19:14 KJV), say it now if you dare; repeat now if you dare your bold presumptuous defiance! What! are you silent? Do you turn your backs and flee? Verily, verily, so was it said of you of old. They that hate him shall flee before him. His enemies shall lick the dust. They shall cry to the rocks to cover them, and to the hills to hide them from his face. How changed, I say, will he be in the appearance of his person.

The difference appears once more in this; he will come again for a very different purpose. He came the first time with, "I delight to do your will, O my God" (Psalm 40:8). He comes a second time to claim the reward and to divide the spoil with the strong. He came the first time with a sin offering; that offering having been once made, there is no more sacrifice for sin. He comes the second time to administer righteousness. He was righteous at his first coming, but it was the righteousness of allegiance. He shall be righteous at his second coming with the righteousness of supremacy. He came to endure the penalty; he comes to procure the reward. He came to serve; he comes to rule. He came to open wide the door of grace; he comes to shut the door. He comes not to redeem but to judge; not to save but to pronounce the sentence; not to weep while he invites, but to smile while he rewards; not to tremble in heart while he proclaims grace, but to make others tremble while he proclaims their doom. Oh Jesus! how great the difference between your first and your second Advent!

Day 25

Behold the Lamb of God

The next day he saw Jesus coming toward him,
and said, "Behold, the Lamb of God,
who takes away the sin of the world!"
John 1:29

When a man says "Behold!" he sees something himself, he sees that something with clearness, and he desires you to see it, and therefore he cries, "Behold! Behold!" John had from his birth been ordained to be the herald of the Christ. But he evidently did not know who the Lamb of God might be. As a babe he leaped in the womb when he came near to the mother of our Lord (Luke 1:44). But yet he did not know Jesus as the Lamb of God. He says, "I myself did not know him" (John 1:31) Some suppose that John and Jesus had never met during their early years, but I find it hard to believe it. I see quite another meaning here.

John knew Jesus but did not know him as the Sin-Bearer. I think he must have known the life of the holy child, his near relative, while he grew in favor both with God and man. But he had not yet seen upon him the attesting seal which marked him as the Son of God. John admired the Lord's character very much, insomuch that when he came to be baptized of him, John said, "I need to be baptized by you" (Matthew 3:14). Yet John says, "I myself did not know him." He knew him as one of high and holy character, but as yet he saw not the token which the Lord God had secretly given to his servant;

for he saw not the Spirit of God descending and resting upon him. John shrewdly suspected that Jesus was the Son of the Highest, of whom he was the forerunner, but a witness must not follow his own surmises, however correct they may be. John, as the Lord's servant, did not dare to know anything of his own unguided judgment. He waited for the secret sign.

Certain preachers tell their people anything they invent out of their wonderful brains; but the true servant of God has no business to put forth his own thoughts or opinions; but he must wait for a word from God. The message should come straight from the Master: "Thus says the Lord." John, though he saw about this wondrous Jesus such marvelous traits of character that he was sure he was much greater than himself, yet says, "I myself did not know him." He would know nothing but as it was revealed to him by the Lord God who sent him.

But when at last he received that personal token, when he plunged our blessed Master into the waters of the Jordan, and saw the heavens opened and the Dove descend, and heard the voice saying, "This is my beloved Son" (Matthew 3:17), then he knew him, and was henceforth sure. When he afterwards spoke he did not say, "I think this is the Lamb of God," or, "I am under the impression that this is the Son of God." No, he boldly cried, "Behold him! See for yourselves. This is the Lamb of God! I speak with the accent of conviction; nothing can shake me. The Master has given the sign, and henceforth I bear confident witness. Behold the Lamb of God, who takes away the sin of the world!"

Henceforth to John the Baptist, the Lord Jesus Christ was more than he appeared to be to any others. To those who looked at the Savior, he would have seemed to be a plain, humble Jew, with nothing particular to mark him out, except it were the gentleness of his demeanor, and a certain heavenliness of carriage. But to the Baptist, he was now before all, and above all. When a person was to be baptized, he confessed his sins to John. But when Jesus came with no sins of his own to confess, did he whisper in John's ear, "I bear the sin of the world"? I think he did; but in any case, this was true to the Baptist's mind, and to him Jesus was henceforth the matchless sacrifice, the one atonement for human sin.

This was an extraordinary truth to John. It took a miracle of grace to make a Jew see, "The Lamb, who takes away the sin of the world." The Jew thought that the sacrifice of God must be for his chosen people only. But John saw beyond all bounds of nationality and restrictions of race, and clearly perceived in Jesus "the Lamb of God, who takes away the sin of the world." Remember that John was of priestly race. He was familiar with lambs for sacrifice. But as a priest, he never saw a lamb for sacrifice in a place far off from the consecrated shrine. There was only one altar, and that was at Jerusalem, and there the lamb of sacrifice must be, and not by Jordan's lonely stream. Yet John saw, in a place never dedicated in any peculiar manner to the service of God, the one great sacrifice standing in the midst of the people. "Behold," says he, "this is the Lamb of God."

Day 26
How God Condemned Sin

For God has done what the law, weakened by the flesh,
could not do. By sending his own Son in the likeness of sinful
flesh and for sin, he condemned sin in the flesh.
Roman 8:3

Ever since man has fallen away from God, two things have been highly desirable. The one, that he should be forgiven all his offenses; the other, equally if not more important, that he should be led to hate the sin into which he has fallen, and love the purity and holiness from which he has become alienated. These two disabilities must be removed; or, looking at the matter from a loftier point of view, these two purposes of divine mercy must be accomplished together. It would be impossible to make a man happy unless both be equally and simultaneously realized. If his sins were forgiven, and yet he loved sin, his prospects would still be dark; over his future the direst portents would loom. If he ceased to love Sin, and yet were still lying under the guilt of it, his present condition would rather be deeply miserable than happy—his conscience pure and sensitive being tortured with pangs of remorse. By what process can the two requirements be met, or the double purpose be achieved? To use our common words, how can man be both justified and sanctified, obtain clearance from his guilt in the sight of God, and then be made holy and meet to appear in his presence?

Human reason suggests that a law should be given to man which he should keep. This has been tried, and the law which was given was the best law that could be framed. The law of God written on the conscience, of which the law given by Moses recorded in the book of Exodus is but a copy, is a perfect law. There is not a command in it that could be omitted; there is not one single arbitrary precept. The right must be true, the true must be right, and God's law is never otherwise than right and true.

But because of our flesh and our tendency to sin, our weakness and our defilement of nature, it could not do what, indeed, God never intended it should do, but what some have thought law might do, to repair the breach and to renovate the depraved. The principle of law, which is, "Do this and you shall be rewarded," or, "Do that and you shall be punished," never can by any means achieve either of these two purposes. The law cannot forgive past sin. It evidently has nothing to do with that question. The law says, "The soul who sins shall die" (Ezekiel 18:20). It can execute the sentence, but it can do no more. It ceases to be law if it lays aside the sword, and does not exact its own penalty.

Yet it has been thought that surely law might make men love holiness, albeit experience and observation prove that it never has that effect. Very often men have needed nothing more than the knowledge of sin to draw them of it, and they have loved sin all the better for knowing it to be sin. If a man sees a thing to be law, he wants to break that law. Because of the evil, as well as the infirmity of our flesh, the mere principle of law will never do anything to purify or ennoble our moral nature. Something more is wanted than merely to shout into men's ears what they ought to be, and what they ought to do. Now, in the text, we are told how God interposed to do by his grace what his law could not do.

We believe in one God, but though we understand not the mystery of the Divine Existence, we accept the propositions declared in Scripture, clearly apprehending the obvious sense of the terms employed, and heartily assenting to the truth of the facts revealed. Thus we believe that the Father is God, and the Son is God, and the Holy Ghost is God, and we worship these three as the one God, the triune God of Israel. The second person of that blessed unity in Trinity was sent by the Father to this earth. He is God the Father's Son, "the only begotten of the Father" (John 1:14 kjv). What that means we do not attempt to define: of the matter of fact, we feel no doubt; of the manner thereof, we can offer no explanation. We suppose that the relationship implied in the words "Father" and "Son" is the nearest description that the Divine Mind can present to our feeble intelligence of that ineffable fellowship, but we do not assume therefore that it explains to us anything, or was intended to explain anything as the basis of an argument, or of a theory concerning the profound doctrine itself. It is a great mystery. Indeed, were there no mystery in God, he were no God to us; for how then should we fear him with the reverence due unto his name? The fact of there being mysteries should never stagger us, poor worms of a day, when we have to think or speak of the infinitely glorious Jehovah.

So, however, it came to pass, that in the fullness of time God sent his Son. He is called in the text, "his own Son," to distinguish him from us who are only his sons by creation, or his sons by regeneration and adoption. He sent his own Son, and he sent him in the flesh. Jesus Christ, the Son of God, was born into this world. He took upon himself our manhood. The Word was made flesh, and dwelt among us, and the apostles declare that they beheld his glory, the glory as of the only begotten of the Father, full of grace and truth. The text uses very important words. It says that God sent his Son "in the likeness of sinful flesh," not in the likeness of flesh, for that would not be true, but in the same likeness as *our* sinful flesh. He was to all intents and purposes like ourselves, tempted in all points like as we are, though without sin, with all our sinless infirmities, with all our tendencies to suffer, with everything human in him except that which comes to be human through human nature having fallen. He was perfectly man; he was like ourselves; and God sent him in the likeness of sinful flesh.

Though it is eighteen hundred years ago and more, the Christmas bells seem to ring on. The joy of his coming is still in our hearts. He lived here his two or three and thirty years, but he was sent, the text tells us, for a reason which caused him to die. He was sent for sin. This may mean that he was sent to do battle with sin, or that he was sent because sin was in the world; or, best of all, he was sent to be a sin-offering. He was sent that he might be the substitute for sinners. God's great plan was this: that inasmuch as his justice could not overlook sin, and sin must be punished, Jesus Christ should come and take the sin of his people upon himself, and upon the accursed tree, the cross of ignominious note, should suffer what was due on our behalf, and that then through his sufferings the infinite love of God should stream forth without any contravention of his infinite justice. This is what God did. He sent his Son to Bethlehem; he sent his Son to Calvary: he sent his Son down to the grave, and he has now recalled him unto the excellent glory where he sits at the right hand of God.

Day 27

A Christmas Question

For to us a child is born,
to us a son is given.
Isaiah 9:6

If it is so, what then? If it is so, *why am I doubtful today*? Why is my spirit questioning? Why do I not realize the fact? My hearer, if the Son is given to you, how is it that you are this day asking whether you are Christ's, or not? Why do you not labor to make your calling and election sure (2 Peter 1:10)? Why do you tarry in the plains of doubt? I may have a large number of persons here to whom it is a matter of uncertainty as to whether Christ is theirs or not. Oh, my dear readers, rest not content unless you know assuredly that Christ is yours, and that you are Christ's.

Suppose you should see in tomorrow's newspaper that some rich man had left you an immense estate. Suppose, as you read it, you were well aware that the person mentioned was a relative of yours, and that it was likely to be true. It may be you have prepared tomorrow for a family meeting, and you are expecting brother John and sister Mary and their little ones to dine with you. But I very much question whether you would not be away from the head of the table to go and ascertain whether the fact were really so. "Oh," you could say, "I am sure I should enjoy my Christmas dinner all the better if I were quite sure about this matter"; and all day, if you did not go, you would be on the tiptoe of expectation; you would be, as it were, sitting upon pins and needles until you knew whether it were the fact or not.

Now there is a proclamation gone forth today, and it is a true one, too, that Jesus Christ has come into the world to save sinners. The question with you is whether he has saved you, and whether you have an interest in him. I beseech you, give no sleep to your eyes, and no slumber to your eyelids, till you have read your "title clear to mansions in the skies." What, man! shall your eternal destiny be a matter of uncertainty to you? What! is heaven or hell involved in this matter, and will you rest until you know which of these shall be your everlasting portion? Are you content while it is a question whether God loves you, or whether he is angry with you? Can you be easy while you remain in doubt as to whether you are condemned in sin, or justified by faith which is in Christ Jesus? Get up, man. I beseech you by the living God, and by your own soul's safety, get up and read the records. Search and look, and try and test yourself, to see whether it be so or not. For if it be so, why should not we know it? If the Son is given to me, why should not I be sure of it? If the child is born to me, why should I not know it for a certainty, that I may even now live in the enjoyment of my privilege—a privilege, the value of which I shall never know to the full, till I arrive in glory?

Again, if it be so, another question. *Why are we sad?* I am looking upon faces just now that appear the very reverse of gloomy, but mayhap the smile covers an aching heart. Brother and sister, why are we sad this morning, if unto us a child is born, if unto us a Son is given? Hark, hark to the cry! It is "Harvest home! Harvest home!" See the maidens as they dance, and the young men as they make merry. And why is this mirth? Because they are storing the precious fruits of the earth, they are gathering together unto their barns wheat which will soon be consumed. And what, brothers and sisters, have we the bread which endures to eternal life and are we unhappy? Does the worldling rejoice when his corn is increased, and do we not rejoice when, "To us a child is born, and to us a son is given?"

Hark, yonder! What means the firing of the Tower guns? Why all this ringing of bells in the church steeples, as if all London were mad with joy? There is a prince born; therefore there is this salute, and therefore are the bells ringing. Ah, Christians, ring the bells of your hearts, fire the salute of your most joyous songs, "For to us a child is born, to us a son is given." Dance, O my heart, and ring out peals of gladness! You drops of blood within my veins dance every one of you! Oh! all my nerves become harp strings, and let gratitude touch you with angelic fingers! And you, my tongue, shout—shout to his praise who has said to you—"To you a child is born, to you a son is given." Wipe that tear away! Come, stop that sighing! Hush your murmuring. What matters your poverty? "To you a child is born." What matters your sickness? "To you a son is given." What matters your sin? For this child shall take the sin away, and this Son shall wash and make you fit for heaven. I say, if it be so,

Lift up the heart, lift up the voice,
Rejoice aloud! you saints rejoice!

But, once more, if it be so, what then? *Why are our hearts so cold*? and why is it that we do so little for him who has done so much for us? Jesus, are you mine? Am I saved? How is it that I love you so little? Why is it that when I preach I am not more in earnest, and when I pray I am not more intensely fervent? How is it that we give so little to Christ who gave himself for us? How is it that we serve him so sadly who served us so perfectly? He consecrated himself wholly; how is it that our consecration is marred and partial? We are continually sacrificing to self and not to him?

O beloved, yield yourselves up this morning. What have you got in the world? "Oh," says one, "I have nothing; I am poor and penniless, and all but houseless." Give yourself to Christ. You have heard the story of the pupils to a Greek philosopher. On a certain day it was the custom to give to the philosopher a present. One came and gave him gold. Another could not bring him gold but brought him silver. One brought him a robe, and another some delicacy for food. But one of them came up, and said, "Oh, Solon, I am poor, I have nothing to give to you, but yet I will give you something better than all these have given; I give you myself." Now, if you have gold and silver, if you have anything of this world's goods, give in your measure to Christ; but take care, above all, that you give yourself to him.

Day 28

A Great Sermon
by the Greatest Preacher

And behold, a voice from heaven said,
"This is my beloved Son, with whom I am well pleased."
Matthew 3:17

The past rather than the present, though not to the exclusion of the present, seems to be intended in the Greek word here used: "This is my beloved Son, with whom I *was* well pleased." That is to say, "Before he was born here among men, before his first infant cry was heard at Bethlehem, before he was obedient to his parents at Nazareth, before he toiled in the carpenter's shop, before he had reached the prime of his manhood, and was able to come forth, and to be dedicated to his sacred ministry in the waters of baptism, before that, I was well pleased with him."

Yes, and we must go further back than that; for he "was" before he was here:

> In the beginning was the Word, and the Word
> was with God, and the Word was God. He was
> in the beginning with God. All things were made
> through him, and without him was not any thing
> made that was made. (John 1:1–3)

In those far-distant ages when the worlds were made, when matter and mind were spoken into existence by the creative word, the Father took counsel with his beloved and equal Son. Jesus Christ as well as the Father was infinite wisdom. He balanced the clouds, and weighed the hills, and appointed the waves of the tide, and kindled the light of the sun. He was the Father's Well-Beloved before ever the earth was. Ay! and in those days primaeval, when as yet there was nothing but God—if your imagination can get back to the time when our great sun and the moon and stars slept in the mind of God, like unborn forests in an acorn cup, in that eternity when there was no time, no day, no space, nor anything save God the All-in-All—you will realize that, even then, the Only-begotten was with the Father, and in him the Father was well pleased, for as God is eternal in his being, he is eternal in the trinity of his person. We cannot fully comprehend the great doctrine of the divine Sonship, and the less we pry into it the better; but certain it is that the Sonship of Christ does not imply any second position in order of time. As the Father was ever the Father, so the Son was ever the Son. Before all worlds and time itself, he was with the Father, coequal and coeternal with him.

Now, dear friends, a love which has endured for ever, which even now is eternal, since it had no beginning, and can have no end, this is a mighty love indeed; and it helps to make us wonder all the more that God should so love the world as to give his only-begotten Son, freighted with such love as this, to come down here, and live, and die, that he might save a guilty race that had only just begun, an infant race of a few thousand years. It will for ever be a marvel that the Father should have been willing to sacrifice the Eternal and

Ever-Blessed for the sake of such worthless creatures as these. Let your minds and hearts adoringly dwell, then, on that first view of the text, "This is my beloved Son, with whom I *was* well pleased."

Now read it, "The Father is well pleased with the Lord Jesus Christ *always*." The "I am" of our version, containing, as it does, within itself the "I was" of the original, implies perpetuity and continuity. God the Father is always pleased with his beloved Son. There was never a time when he was otherwise than pleased with him. Ay! he was pleased with him even in Gethsemane, when his sweat was as it were great drops of blood falling to the ground. He was pleased with him when he gave him up to be nailed to the cross of Calvary. For, though it pleased the Father to prove him, and he did for a while hide his face from him because of the necessary purposes of his atoning sacrifice, yet he always loved him. I think that our Lord was never fairer to the eyes of his Father than when he was all ruddy with his bloody sweat, and that he never seemed lovelier to him than when his obedient hands were given to the nails, and his willing feet were fastened to the tree. Then must he have seemed to be God's rose and lily, first spotless, then all blood-stained, the gathering up of all the lovelinesses of which even the infinite mind of God could conceive. The Well-Beloved was always dear to the Father; the Father was always well pleased with him; and he is well pleased with him now.

How little there is even about those of us who are the Lord's children which can please our heavenly Father; but God is always well pleased with Christ. We get wandering away from him; our garments become defiled by sin. Sometimes, the Lord needs to chide us, and to chastise us. But as for his beloved Son, he is always well pleased with him; and, blessed be his name, he is well pleased with us, in him! Oh, that we could always remember this glorious truth! Still, whatever we may be, the finger of the great Father ever points to his dear Son in the glory, and he says, "This, this is my beloved Son, with whom, notwithstanding all that his people do, I am always well pleased."

Day 29

The Power and Wisdom of God

Christ the power of God and the wisdom of God.
1 Corinthians 1:24b

Christ considered as God and man, the Son of God equal with his Father, and yet the man, born of the Virgin Mary. Christ, in his complex person, is "the power of God and the wisdom of God."

He is the power of God from all eternity. "By the word of the Lord the heavens were made, and by the breath of his mouth all their host" (Psalm 33:6). "The Word was with God, and the Word was God. . . . All things were made through him, and without him was not any thing made that was made" (John 1:1, 3). The pillars of the earth were placed in their everlasting sockets by the omnipotent right hand of Christ; the curtains of the heavens were drawn upon their rings of starry light by him who was from everlasting the all-glorious Son of God. The orbs that float aloft in ether, those ponderous planets, and those mighty stars, were placed in their positions or sent rolling through space by the eternal strength of him who is "the first and the last" (Revelation 1:17), "the ruler of kings on earth" (v. 5). Christ is the power of God, for he is the Creator of all things, and by him all things exist.

But when he came to earth, took upon himself the fashion of a man, tabernacled in the inn, and slept in the manger, he still gave proof that he was the Son of

God; not so much so when, as an infant of a span long, the immortal was the mortal and the infinite became a babe; not so much so in his youth, but afterward when he began his public ministry, he gave abundant proofs of his power and Godhead. The winds hushed by his finger uplifted, the waves calmed by his voice, so that they became solid as marble beneath his tread; the tempest, cowering at his feet, as before a conqueror whom it knew and obeyed; these things, these stormy elements, the wind, the tempest, and the water, gave full proof of his abundant power. The lame man leaping, the deaf man hearing, the dumb man singing, the dead rising, these, again, were proofs that he was the "power of God." When the voice of Jesus startled the shades of Hades, and rent the bonds of death, with "Lazarus, come out!" (John 11:43), and when the carcass rotten in the tomb woke up to life, there was proof of his divine power and Godhead. A thousand other proofs he afforded; but we need not stay to mention them to you who have Bibles in your houses, and who can read them every day. At last, he yielded up his life, and was buried in the tomb. Not long, however, did he sleep; for he gave another proof of his divine power and Godhead, when starting from his slumber, he terrified the guards with the majesty of his grandeur, not being held by the bonds of death, they being like the fresh bowstrings before our conquering Samson (Judges 16:7–9), who had meanwhile pulled up the gates of hell, and carried them on his shoulders far away (Judges 16:3).

That he is the power of God now, Scripture very positively affirms; for it is written, "he is seated at the right hand of God" (Colossians 3:1). He has the reins of Providence gathered in his hands; the fleet coursers of Time are driven by him who sits in the chariot of the world, and bids its wheels run round; and he shall bid them stay when it shall please him. He is the great umpire of all disputes, the great Sovereign Head of the church, the Lord of heaven, and death, and hell; and by-and-by we shall know that he shall come,

On fiery clouds and wings of wind,
Appointed judge of all mankind;

and then the quickened dead, the startled myriads, the divided firmaments, the "Depart from me, you cursed," and the "Come, you who are blessed" (Matthew 25:41, 34), shall proclaim him to be the power of God, who has power over all flesh, to save or to condemn, as it pleases him.

But he is equally "the wisdom of God." The great things that he did before all worlds were proofs of his wisdom. He planned the way of salvation; he devised the system of atonement and substitution; he laid the foundations of the great plan of salvation. There was wisdom. But he built the heavens by wisdom, and he laid the pillars of light, whereon the firmament is balanced, by his skill and wisdom. Mark the world; and learn, as you see all its multitudinous proofs of the wisdom of God, and there you have the wisdom of Christ; for he was the creator of it.

And when he became a man, he gave proofs enough of wisdom. Even in childhood, when he made the doctors sit abashed by the questions that he asked, he showed that he was more than mortal. And when the Pharisee and Sadducee and Herodian were all at last defeated, and their nets were broken, he proved again the superlative wisdom of the Son of God. And when those who came to take him, stood enchained by his eloquence, spellbound by his marvelous oratory, there was again a proof that he was the wisdom of God, who could so enchain the minds of men.

And now that he intercedes before the throne of God, now that he is our Advocate before the throne, the pledge and surety for the blessed, now that the reins of government are in his hands, and are ever wisely directed, we have abundant proofs that the wisdom of God is in Christ, as well as the power of God. Bow before him, you that love him! Bow before him, you that desire him! Crown him, crown him, crown him! He is worthy of it, unto him is everlasting might; unto him is unswerving wisdom. Bless his name! Exalt him! Clap your wings, you seraphs! Cry aloud, you cherubim! Shout, shout, shout, to his praise, you ransomed host above! And you, O men and women that know his grace, extol him in your songs forever, for he is Christ, the power of God and the wisdom of God.

Day 30

The End Is Better

Better is the end of a thing than its beginning.
Ecclesiastes 7:8

This year has all but gone—1864, then, must soon be numbered with the things that were. Perhaps someone says, "Would to God that I had this year to live over again! I have missed many opportunities of doing good. Or, when I have availed myself of them, I have not served my God as I could have desired. I have another year left in which to serve the Church, the world, and my God. I have spent another of my talents, and have so, much fewer to put out to usury for my Lord and Master."

Now, do not regret, dear friend, that the year has passed. It should be rather to you, if you are a believer in Christ, a subject for congratulation. Would you wish to have the year over again, when in sober silence you meditate upon the subject? You have had some sorrows this year. You are like the sailor I spoke of just now; you have passed through some storms. Weather-beaten mariner, would you like to have the storms of this year over again? Do you remember that dreadful night when the ship was driven so fearfully by the tempest, or the time when you were cast upon the rocks? Would you like to endure the same again? I see you shake your head, and say, "No; thank God we weathered that storm. But we don't want it again." And, Christians, as you think of the losses, crosses, sufferings, and bereavements which you have had during this year, can you feel any regret that it is gone?

How many snares have you escaped during the past year? In looking back, must you not observe that your feet have sometimes almost gone, and your steps have nearly slipped? There have been times when sin had almost tripped you up, when the world had almost taken you in its trap, and when the devil had all but wounded you in a mortal part. You are like a sailor who remembers the rocks by which he has sailed, and the quicksand from which he has escaped. Would you wish to run such risks again? And are you not grateful, Christian, that another year of temptation has gone forever, and that the arrows that Satan has shot at you this year, he can shoot at you no more forever? Those, sword-cuts we received, which threatened to be mortal, we shall never have to dread again; they are gone. And when I say they are gone, it is implied that their mischief and their power to hurt are gone for over.

But there is another side to this matter. What a multitude of mercies you have enjoyed this year! How good God has been to us!

When all your mercies, O my God,
My rising soul surveys;
Transported with the view, I'm lost
In wonder, love, and praise.

Those of us who have traveled in Switzerland, or in other countries where the views are glorious to look upon, would not wish that we had never seen them; on the contrary, we are glad that our eyes have feasted on those sunny prospects. And you, too, Christian, cannot regret that you have seen God's mercies, but you will thank God that it has been your privilege to have enjoyed such favors.

There is another reason, then, why you should not regret that the year has passed. I address myself to some who are growing grey. I know there is a tendency in your minds to regret that so many years have gone; but, my dear brothers and sisters in the Lord, if you should do so, I think you would be guilty of a folly unworthy of a believer with such a long experience. Take John Bunyan's picture of the Christian's progress. He describes Christian as starting on his pilgrimage to the Celestial City with a burden on his back that pressed him down. Wringing his hands for fear, and running back, he is afraid that he will be destroyed in the City of Destruction. He has not gone a day's journey before he is up to his neck in the Slough of Despond, and floundering in the mire. This is the beginning of the pilgrimage but see the end: he has come to the river, he dips his foot into it, and though it is chill and cold, it does not stay him. When he gets midway in the river, how does Bunyan picture him? The angels beckon him from the other side, those very angels whose voices he had heard ringing clear and sweet across the stream, when he wandered in the groves of Beulah, and sat among the spices there. And now he reaches the bank on the other side, and, leaving his sins, his doubts, his infirmities, his mortality behind, his disembodied spirit goes up to the celestial land, and angel attendants conduct him to the pearly gates of the golden-paved city. Oh! infinitely better is the end of a spiritual life than the beginning. Contrast the Slough of Despond with the Celestial City, and human intellect cannot fail to see how much better, how infinitely better, the end is than the beginning.

Take this picture as a further illustration of the same point: Moses at the beginning of his spiritual career is seen killing an Egyptian and burying him in the sand (Exodus 2:12)—just like a young Christian, full of zeal, but having little prudence. There is the beginning of his public career. And now I think I see the old man of 120 years, firm of step, with an eye as clear and piercing as an eagle's, standing up to address the people whom he has carried, as nursing mother, in his arms; and, having done this, leaving Joshua, his familiar servant, and all others behind, he began to climb to the top of Pisgah. He has mounted to its loftiest crag, and, leaning over, he begins to take a full view of the Promised Land. He sees the palm trees of Jerusalem and Zion, and his eye lingers on Bethlehem; he catches glimpses of the blue sea afar off, and the goodly land of Lebanon; and as he looks, one scene melts into the other, and he sees the face of God, for God himself has come down, and his spirit is taken away with a kiss. As to his body, it is buried where no man knows; but as to his soul, it is with God for ever (Deuteronomy 34:1–7).

Truly, in the case of Moses, the end was better than the beginning, and such shall be the spiritual end of every man of God who, with the simplicity and faith of Moses, shall put his faith in God. I think this is sufficient to soothe all your regret. Instead of being sorry that these years have passed, thank God for it, and be glad.

Acknowledgments

This project came together thanks to Brad Byrd, Ruth Castle, and the team at New Growth Press. I'm also thankful for Jason Allen and the trustees at Midwestern Baptist Theological Seminary for their vision to promote Spurgeon's writings and resources for the church, for the saints at Wornall Road Baptist Church, and for my assistants David Aust, Isaac Pang, Aaron Day, and the rest of the team at the Spurgeon Library, who helped me with research, compiling, and editing.

As with every other Spurgeon-related project I've worked on, it has been a rich privilege to study and share my findings from the life and works of Charles Spurgeon. I'm grateful to God for the opportunity to do so. May he be glorified in his Son, world without end.